MY NEW TABLE

MY NEW TABLE

Everyday Inspiration for Eating + Living

Trish Magwood

Photography by Ksenija Hotic

appetite

by RANDOM HOUSE

Appetite by Random House® and colophon are registered
trademarks of Penguin Random House LLC.

Library and Archives Canada Cataloguing in Publication is
available upon request.

ISBN: 978-0-525-61124-0
eBook ISBN: 978-0-525-61125-7

Photography by Ksenija Hotic
Food and prop styling by Trish Magwood
Additional styling by Ksenija Hotic
Book and cover design by Jennifer Griffiths
Printed and bound in China

Published in Canada by Appetite by Random House®,
a division of Penguin Random House Canada Limited.

www.penguinrandomhouse.ca

10 9 8 7 6 5 4 3 2 1

appetite
by RANDOM HOUSE

For Fin, Olivia, and Charlotte, my most favourite and important mouths to feed and my most cherished table companions. For Peter, the most entertaining person to share any table with. For Mom and Dad, the people who showed me the importance of connection, family, and all gatherings. And for my extended family, I will always choose you as the ones to gather around my new table.

CONTENTS

INTRODUCTION

My table has seen it all. In my twenties, it saw me through my first job at a magazine and then at chef school, learning the food and media trade. It saw me launching my own business, *dish*, a cooking school, retail store, café, catering business, and lifestyle brand. In my thirties, it's where I fed and raised my three children, Fin, Olivia, and Charlotte—the loves of my life. With them, I have had my happiest and most memorable times. My table has also watched me embark on exciting new opportunities like hosting and producing television shows, writing and publishing two cookbooks, and selling my business. In my forties, my table was always there during the many fun and amazing moments and rewarding work projects, and it also stood sturdy through times of uncertainty and change. It was there when my mom beat cancer. And it was my anchor through the difficult, lonely, and terrifying times when I got separated and divorced. In the toughest moments, there were times I stayed away from the cooking I loved so dearly, but I always found my way back again, thanks to my happy, resilient kids, incredible parents, and dear friends. And then I met Peter, and we have fun and he makes me laugh.

Now, as I arrive at my fiftieth birthday, my table is different, ever-changing, growing, and wonderful—at times it's our combined five kids, with Peter's children Connor and Emma, and other favourite regulars too. But it is also still familiar, as we collectively hold onto the traditions that keep our evolving families connected and together. Through all the changes at my table, the idea for this cookbook has been a constant. With food, I find a sense of purpose and meaning, and accomplishment. I have long wanted to share the simple recipes that are a mainstay for my family, while also showing how the food on the table can bring the ones you love together. In that way, I see

this as a cookbook of family recipes, for however you define family. For me, family is large, robust, evolving, flexible, growing, hungry, and happy—requiring recipes that are casual and easy for time-pressed, busy nights.

I also wanted to create a look-book, to share the places and things that make me happy. And so this is a visual, photo-driven book to give you the chance to dream or escape a little (thanks to my photographer, Ksenija's fabulous photos) as well as to find renewed joy in the comforts of home. And there couldn't have been a better time to write it. While this book was lovingly being created, I was also moving my kids from the family home they grew up in to a new shared home with Peter. We embarked on a full renovation adventure at our new place, spanning a year of change and happy chaos, to turn it into a home for all of us. This book, like the renovation, became a project for the whole family, with my kids and my mom testing the recipes, my dad editing them, and all of us sitting together to eat (and critique and improve and retest) the meals you'll find in these pages.

As I was adapting to what my table means to me now, I was also trying to define it on the page, through the words and photographs in this book. And what I discovered is that my new table is much as it ever has been: the place where we can gather to eat, share stories, and connect with and love each other deeply.

None of us could have imagined the events of this past year, or that the world would be turned upside down. I believe, as the world has lost and grieved and feared and learned, we have gained a new awareness about our need to connect with family and friends. And a renewed appreciation for the importance of getting outside to move and walk. Through necessity, we had to retreat more inside our homes—our nests—and the vital importance of having a comforting place for family to spend the days together became ever more clear.

My hope is that you may all find your version of a happy table. I would love for you to use this book to help define your table, your rituals, your style—so that in these changing times, we can have an anchor and a place to connect; somewhere to find joy and create meaning with those we hold most dear.

May you enjoy *My New Table*, and may it inspire you and help you define your table, wherever and whatever it may be. With much gratitude and appreciation, I am so happy to share it with you.

CITY + COUNTRY

I live my life with one shoe in the city, and one boot on the farm; between the bustling energy of Toronto, and the calmer, much smaller town of Creemore, Ontario. Life in the city offers unique, vibrant neighbourhoods and parks, restaurants, shops and culture, and a community of incredible friends. It's exciting and energizing. Life in the country offers beautiful landscapes, outdoor and farm living, and tightknit communities. Country life reminds you to have an appreciation for the simpler things. I have been fortunate enough to be shaped by both.

Growing up, my family's school and work life in the busy city was balanced with the ritual of us piling into the car and heading up north to the country on weekends and holidays. Thanks to my grandparents' influence, we embraced the outdoor lifestyle no matter where we were. In the winter, we'd downhill ski, ride horses on snowy trails, go to outdoor football games no matter how chilly it was, or take trips to Quebec for Carnival. In the summer, my brothers and I would be by the water, whether we were at summer camp or at the cottage. We'd also get the most out of the beautiful Bruce Trail—the longest marked trail in Canada—with its seemingly endless hiking, cross-country skiing, and yak tracking.

When we were older, my parents purchased a farm near Creemore, a quaint and pretty village. The farm has a large vegetable garden, a fruit orchard, and a vineyard, which have all become sources of inspiration for me. For friends and family, my parents host annual maple-syrup making in their sugar bush and share honey from their beehives. They have a pond that freezes into the best skating rink in the winter and melts to become the perfect place to swim in the heat of the summer. Gathering outdoors is a natural part of our lives.

Creemore has become our family hub. My kids and I are lucky to be there all the time, and happily and naturally call it home. My brothers and their families also have places nearby. It's not unusual for 12 cousins to be together. And when I first met Peter, through mutual friends in the Creemore area, we immediately bonded over our shared desire to spend as much time as possible in the country, and at his beautiful place. I love how we gather at friends' places, around the farmers' market, and at local restaurants in Creemore.

The kids and I travel between Toronto and Creemore often, as do Peter and his kids. Toronto offers the perks of city living. Creemore, with its small-town spirit, feeds my need for moments with my family and for being part of a warm community. Both city and country have shaped my connection with food and lifestyles. Seeing how my parents live on the farm, and the care they take in growing their produce, has cemented my appreciation for local, in-season food—while there, we eat simply and seasonally and often at the grill. And when I'm in the city, I love the ritual of dinners at our favourite family-run restaurants and the adventure of trying small, up-and-coming new places, as well as the comfort of supporting my local grocers and butchers. If you ask me, a change in settings is the best medicine for stress and restlessness. So I'll keep one shoe in the city, and one boot on the farm.

HOME ESSENTIALS

I think I've always loved design as much as food. To me, they're intertwined, part of the same lifestyle; both about the importance of the home front. While I have no official design credentials, over the years, through various projects and learning tips and tricks from talented experts, I suppose I've earned some street cred. I've learned to trust my gut, be brave in breaking rules, authentic to my love of mixing old with new, and, most importantly, to stay true to my family's collective needs. I approached the design of our new home in Toronto the same way I approach my cooking: keep it simple, less is more. I believe you should curate your home, and be selective and discerning about what you choose to put in it. Splurge on a few pieces that will truly define the space, and stick to more reasonably priced options for the stuff that's seasonal or will need to be replaced often. A home should reflect the personalities of the people who live there, and work for the way you live. When you get that balance right, every spot will resonate in a way that makes it *feel* like home.

Each room and every nook of your home should make you feel calm, which to me means uncluttered. Anyone who knows me knows I'm a neat freak. I can't help it. The canvas—whether it's the front hall, the kitchen counter, or my desk—needs to look orderly for me to have any sense of calm. I will wipe the counter under you while you're eating at it. On the flip side, I don't care if you traipse through the house in your shoes—so long as I can't see the dirt. I know my neat obsession is mine alone, but I hope those I live with appreciate it a little . . . or may one day?

After years of practice, I have learned certain things about organizing a busy home and kitchen with hungry kids and friends coming and going, in a way that answers my need for neatness. Here are some tips and tricks I used when setting up each area of our new house.

FRONT HALL

The front hall is a drop zone for mail, keys, wallets, sunglasses, baseball hats, and hair elastics. My first challenge was to accept that this is how we live. My next was to make the hallway functional yet pretty. To do that, I found some creative hide-the-crap dishes and boxes.

With seven people under our roof at times, I try to limit each of us to keeping only a single pair of shoes in the hall. The rest go in the closet. I'm not sure anyone realizes this is the rule . . . Or notices that I move their shoes to the closet many times a day. If you have the space, a bench can do double duty in a hall: a place to keep shoes neatly tucked away and somewhere to sit while you tie your laces before you head out the door.

POWDER ROOM

Powder rooms often open up to kitchens or living rooms, for the whole world to see. I recommend you keep the door closed and add a cute sign. Splurge on conversational wallpaper and some nice hand soap and towels for when guests do go inside (and maybe judge). Think of the powder room as a miniature showcase for your entire home.

LIVING ROOM

Growing up, living rooms were formal, uncomfortable, and often unused. Today the living room is the room we live in. Seating should be welcoming, comfortable, and able to seat family and friends. Coffee and side tables should be pretty but also functional to hold drinks and snacks.

LIGHTING

Table and standing lights are pretty and can be necessary complements to the backdrop of pot lights; sconces, and wall-mounted lights can define a space. Dimmers are critical to crank up when reading and dim down for ambient gatherings or movie watching. I am forever fiddling with the dimmers to create the mood that suits the time of day.

KITCHEN SINK

Usually the sink area is the centrepiece of your kitchen, so treat it like art and pick a beautiful faucet (see mine on page 12). Store ugly brushes and cloths in a unique vessel like handmade pottery or keep them hidden under the sink.

KITCHEN COUNTERS

Pare down what you keep on the counter to maximize your prep space and give the kitchen a feeling of calm. A good selection of wooden spoons along with your other most-used cook's tools is all you need stove-side. Add a pretty tray for essential ingredients (oils, salt, pepper) if there's not a cupboard within reach for these.

KITCHEN STORAGE

Practical storage is a must for me. I have various sizes of pull-out drawers for large, heavy appliances and containers, vertical slats for sheet pans, and fixed shelves for easy visibility. Your drawers or shelves for dishes should be within reach of the dishwasher. A dish drawer makes setting the table and unloading the dishwasher a snap. It's decadent for knives to have their own drawer, but as the key tool in the kitchen they deserve the real estate. Place knives on a rubber mat to keep them organized and make them easy to grab.

STOVE TOWEL BAR

My grandmother's rule for the stove's towel bar was one hand towel for hands, one dish towel for dishes. Sometimes I have well-used utilitarian dish towels on the go, other times I put out special-occasion towels just for show.

OPEN SHELVES

If you want to lighten up the feel of your kitchen, consider removing the cupboard doors and adding tiles or a fresh coat of paint to the back cupboard walls. Floating shelves can be beautiful (so long as you don't display your chipped mugs and collection of university beer glasses on them). Or put glass doors on cupboards to showcase your pretty things. Items like booze bottles and old candles can be kept hidden behind closed doors.

COFFEE STATION

When organizing your kitchen, consider your breakfast needs. We have a coffee station with a coffee maker, mugs, and fixings. I place the toaster, breadboard, and butter dish in the same nook to make tired mornings as easy as possible.

DESK

When we renovated our home, I made sure to keep a spot for my desk in the kitchen because I constantly go back and forth between the computer and the kitchen. The kitchen also has the best source of light, making it easy to work. This central location means I can work alongside my kids, who prefer to do their homework at the kitchen counter or table despite having desks in their rooms. To keep your desk organized, a drawer for pens and pencils is key. With paperwork, I continue to surprise myself (and horrify my dad) that I am a piler and not a filer—contrary to my neat-freak status. I use a desktop file organizer for bits and pieces of bills and mail. A grommet hole to hide your computer and phone chords minimizes clutter. And a little tray to hold a candle, or whatever else makes you feel calm, is a worthwhile addition.

DINING COLLECTIBLES AND SERVING WARE

It takes time to collect entertaining and serving essentials. Less is more, though, so don't rush to fill the gaps. Wait for the right pieces to come along. Maybe a water pitcher carried home from your travels, a board you discovered in an antique shop, the glasses from your wedding, or a platter gifted from a grandmother. I love to mix and match natural wood textures with unique shapes and colours of ceramics. Combine old and new to find your own personal style. Care for them, display them, and use them.

LINENS

Like serving ware, linens are best collected over time. I've collected tea towels from some of my favourite kitchen shops in London and Napa, and I smile every time I pull them out. Linens can be a statement of your personal style. My old neighbourhood friends, Ghislaine and Liz, use bright colours and bold patterns daily, and both their indoor and outdoor tables always look fresh and vibrant. Fellow chef and cookbook author Laura Calder has an enviable French linen collection for her Fancy Fridays, and has even turned some into dresses. I like to mix and match like colours and patterns, using casual, easy-to-clean placements for the everyday, and special placemats and napkins to suit the occasion. I'll use my grandmother's old fancy linen for a girls' lunch. Or tea towels in place of napkins when I know things are going to get messy.

THE TABLE

Setting the table is one of the best tasks for kids to do from an early age. It helps them appreciate the sense of occasion that can come from sitting together to share a meal. Long gone are the days when I plated the dinner in the kitchen to make sure vegetables were on the kids' plates. Now—with a large crowd at most dinners—I set the food out family-style for people to help themselves. I use wooden boards underneath hot dishes and serve food in pretty bowls to make every meal special. And I place a few water jugs on the table so no one has to jump up for drinks.

If you want your dinner crowd to linger longer, get cozy with blankets and cushions or sheepskins. Dimmed lights, music, and candles make every dinner feel like a special occasion. And living stuff—like a little plant or herb box on the table—adds a warm and natural touch.

COOKING ESSENTIALS

I'm a butter-and-olive-oil, salt-and-pepper kind of cook. I believe in using simple, good-quality ingredients and letting their natural flavours shine. Wherever possible, I shop and eat seasonally and locally—asparagus in the spring; peas, and beans in early summer; tomatoes and corn at the end of summer; apples, pears and squashes in the fall; and sweet potatoes and other earthy root vegetables in early winter. I encourage you to find and support your own local, small farms and producers. Not only will you develop a deeper appreciation for the food you eat, but your family, friends, and guests will thank you for the taste. I buy my meat from a trusted butcher who can tell me where the meat is from. I try to buy organic and local cuts that are antibiotic- and hormone-free. I shop at a trusted fishmonger and prepare the fish the day I buy it.

Over the years, what I cook and eat has changed, and these days I take a more vegetable-forward approach. I start by thinking about seasonal salads and sides when I'm grocery shopping or preparing a meal, and then I choose a simple grilled or roasted protein that will complement the vegetables. You'll see the recipes in this book are produce-led, usually following the rhythm of the seasons, and that they are quick and simple for the most part. My hope is that they will make it easy for you to decide what the heck to make for dinner. But food is personal. We all have different palates, and my recipes reflect my own tastes. You'll notice I don't use a lot of garlic—it gives me a food hangover. And I don't cook a lot with legumes or whole grains, despite their redeeming qualities, because they hurt my belly. Oh, and I really dislike truffle oil and cilantro, so those don't get a look here. But it's your table, your palate, so please add, subtract, and adapt to your liking. Think of my recipes as guides and modify them to suit your preferences and inspiration to change up your repertoire.

Essential Ingredients

Here's a list of my cooking and baking essentials, including my favourite brands, where I think it's important to note them. When you're shopping for essentials, organize your shopping list according to the aisles in the grocery store and you'll be out of there in no time.

PANTRY

› Artisinal breads (Blackbird or Collingwood Bread Company) and crackers are always on hand (I love Lesley Stowe Raincoast Crisps).

› Coconut milk

› Dried spices: cayenne, chili flakes, curry, steak spice blend, za'atar

› Maple syrup and honey (our own Magwood brand)

› Mustards: Dijon, dried, grainy (Kozlik's Canadian Triple Crunch is perfect), Russian sweet

› Nuts + seeds: almonds, cashews, peanuts, pistachios, walnuts, chia seeds, flaxseeds, pepitas, poppy seeds, sesame seeds, sunflower seeds

› Oils: avocado, coconut, or grapeseed (for high heat sautéing); extra virgin olive oil (I like first pressed Napa Valley Olive Oil, and Colin Webster's from Siurana, Spain)

› Pasta, rice + grains: fusilli, penne, spaghetti, tagliatelle; Arborio, basmati, brown, jasmine; farro, quinoa

› Peppercorns (good-quality, for freshly cracked pepper using a peppermill)

› Peppers: jalapeno, peperoncini piccanti (I like Terroni), red pepper jam (my own)

› Salts: fine sea salt (for daily seasoning), flaked Maldon sea salt (for daily finishing), French Grey and pink Himalayan (for special finishing)

› Sauces + pastes: hot sauce, soy sauce, sriracha, tomato sauce (I like Raos, and always keep San Marzano tomatoes on hand), harissa, Thai curry paste (red or green)

› Stock (or broth): beef, chicken, vegetable

› Vinegars: aged balsamic from Modena; cider, red wine, sherry, white wine

› Wine: when a recipe calls for wine, use whatever you have on hand (except for sweet wine)—which for me is usually Chablis—if it's not good enough to drink, it's not good enough to cook with

BAKING

> All-purpose unbleached flour

> Baking powder

> Baking soda

> Chocolate chips: dark, bitter, semisweet

> Cinnamon: ground

> Cocoa powder

> Coconut: shredded, unsweetened

> Ginger: fresh

> Molasses

> Oats: old-fashioned rolled

> Pure honey (I like natural and local, like our own Magwood Honey by Osprey Beekeeper)

> Pure maple syrup (natural and local, like our Magwood Maple Syrup by Badjeros Mennonite Farmer, or Four Wheel Farm Maple Syrup by Chuck Magwood)

> Pure vanilla extract

> Sugars: granulated, brown, cane (I use granulated throughout the recipes)

FRIDGE

> Butter: although most experts suggest cooking with unsalted butter so you can control the amount of salt, I grew up with salted butter and it's what we love in our house (we use Stirling)

> Cheese: raw and pasteurized cow, goat, or sheep; a mix of hard such as Parmesan or asiago, semisoft such as ricotta or Gorgonzola, and triple cream such as Delice de Bourgogne or brie (for cheese boards); some recipes show cheese by package weight (grams) with imperial conversions (ounces)

> Cream and milk: whipping and 10%; milk of your choice (I use 1%)

> Eggs: free-range, farm-named large eggs (I like Rowe Farms eggs)

> Fresh herbs

> Lemons and limes: I don't get too exact but as a good guide, 1 lemon yields about ¼ cup juice and 1 tablespoon zest; 1 lime yields about 2 tablespoons juice and 2 teaspoons zest

> Yogurt: Greek and plain, and always full-fat

Essential Tools

COOKING + SERVING

› Aluminum foil and parchment paper

› Barbecue utensils: flipper, tongs, and scrub brush

› Blenders: Vitamix for smoothies, immersion for soups

› Coffee grinder and French press

› Cooking dishware: casserole and gratin dishes

› Cooking utensils: colander, flippers, garlic press, ladles, mandoline (it makes slicing thinly easy, but a knife will work too), potato masher, rasp or grater, spatulas, tongs, wooden spoons, y-peeler)

› Knives (I use chef's knives most frequently—for chopping and dicing, paring knives for small detail work, utility knives for general use, carving knives for meats, and bread knives)

› Pans: general nonstick (I like Green Pan); stainless steel straight-sided sauté and fry (I like All-Clad); sheet and roasting pans; an old cast-iron skillet

› Pots: pasta/stockpot with lid, small saucepan, 4-quart and 6-quart pots with lids (I like All-Clad)

› Salt and pepper mills and salt dish

› Scissors

› Serving bowls and dishes: small for mis en place; assorted other sizes and styles

› Serving ware: assorted spoons

› Wooden cutting boards

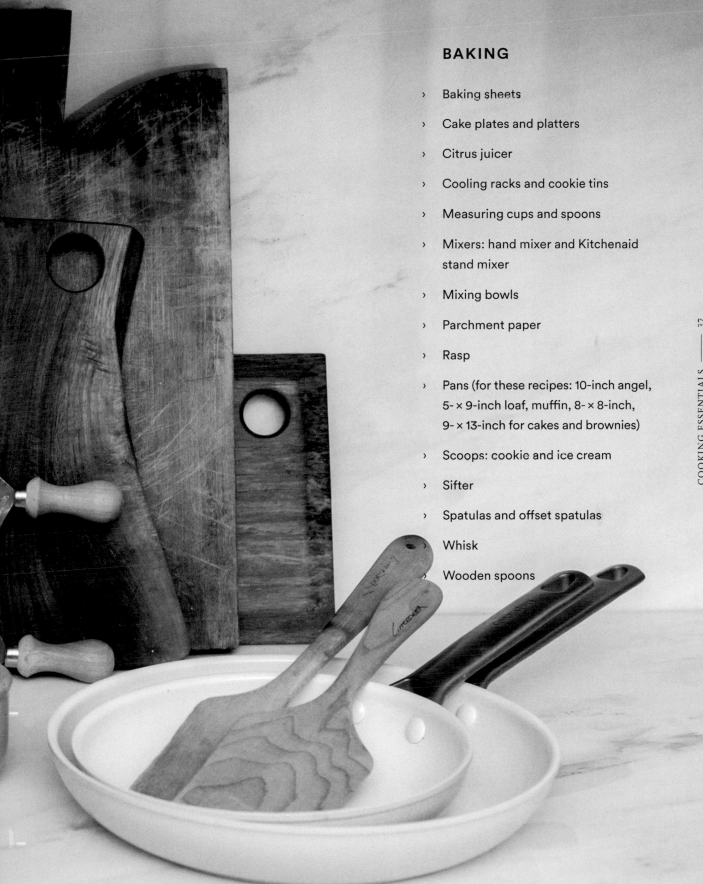

BAKING

› Baking sheets

› Cake plates and platters

› Citrus juicer

› Cooling racks and cookie tins

› Measuring cups and spoons

› Mixers: hand mixer and Kitchenaid stand mixer

› Mixing bowls

› Parchment paper

› Rasp

› Pans (for these recipes: 10-inch angel, 5- × 9-inch loaf, muffin, 8- × 8-inch, 9- × 13-inch for cakes and brownies)

› Scoops: cookie and ice cream

› Sifter

› Spatulas and offset spatulas

› Whisk

› Wooden spoons

SNACKS

PICKLED CUCUMBERS

My Grandma Bo used to pickle field cucumbers to go with her classic roast beef dinner, and she'd always peel them first. They were a favourite for my brother Jeff and me—but there were rarely enough to go round, so a mild panic usually ensued. I use readily available English cucumbers instead, which I don't bother to peel. And I make sure there's enough to go round.

MAKES ABOUT 4 CUPS

INGREDIENTS

2 English cucumbers (or 8 mini field cucumbers)

½ cup white vinegar

2 tsp fine sea salt

Freshly cracked pepper

2 Tbsp peppercorns (optional)

2 Tbsp chopped dill (optional)

HOW TO

Slice the cucumbers very thinly. Place in a sealable jar or bowl, cover with the vinegar and salt, and season with pepper. Add the peppercorns and dill (if using), then seal the jar. Refrigerate for at least 1 hour before serving. Store, sealed, in the fridge for up to 2 days.

PICKLED ONIONS

I'm taking some liberties with the term "pickled" here. One of my favourite cookbook chefs, Yotam Ottolenghi, takes the proper approach to pickling onions: he boils aromatics in water, removes them from the heat, adds cider vinegar and honey, and then pickles his onions. I love Ottolenghi's restaurants, books, and recipes, but I can't be bothered pickling onions the classic way. I take a less fussy approach and pickle mine in lime juice. The result is beautiful, vibrant pink onions with a soft texture and lovely pickled flavour.

MAKES ABOUT 2 CUPS

INGREDIENTS

1 large red onion

½ tsp fine sea salt

Juice of 2 limes

HOW TO

Slice the onion very thinly. Place in an airtight 2-cup sealable jar and sprinkle with the salt. Cover with the lime juice, add 1 tablespoon of water, lightly stir to combine, and seal the jar. Refrigerate for at least 1 hour before serving. Store, sealed, in the fridge for up to 2 days.

COOK'S NOTE

Pickled Onions are the perfect accompaniment to tacos (page 192), burgers (page 227), and grilled fish or meat. They're also a great addition to salads, especially those with cheese, to balance the fat and acid.

PICKLED JALAPENOS

The Scoville scale ranks peppers according to their heat units from 0 to 16 million. At the low end of the scale are bell peppers, moving through peperoncini, ancho, jalapeno, serrano, cayenne, and Scotch bonnet, all the way up to pure capsaicin. There's an ongoing heat-tolerance competition in our house. I love jalapenos. Fin likes to live on the edge with tabasco peppers. Wherever you land on the heat scale, most peppers taste great pickled. We gobble them up as pizza toppings and alongside mains. I can't make them fast enough to keep up with demand. With this recipe, you can swap a few of the jalapenos out for tabasco and Hungarian wax peppers. Or try doubling the sugar for candied pickled jalapenos.

MAKES ABOUT 4 CUPS

INGREDIENTS

8 jalapenos	3 Tbsp sugar
1 cup white vinegar	2 Tbsp fine sea salt
1 cup water	4 cloves garlic, smashed

HOW TO

Preheat the oven to 400°F. Wash and dry four 1-cup wide-mouth mason jars and place on a sheet pan, alongside their lids, all face up. Heat in the oven for 15 minutes to sterilize. Wearing gloves, use a paring knife to trim the stems off the jalapenos. Slice the jalapenos into rings, keeping the seeds in place.

In a medium pot, bring the vinegar, water, sugar, salt, and garlic to a boil. When the sugar and salt have dissolved, remove from the heat. Let cool for a few minutes. Add the sliced jalapenos and let the mixture cool completely. After 10 to 15 minutes, they will start to turn an olive colour.

Using tongs, remove the jalapenos from the liquid and pack them into the prepared jars. Using a funnel placed over the openings of the jars, ladle the pickling liquid overtop, leaving a little space at the top of the jars, then seal. Store sealed in the fridge for up to 3 days. They will lose their colour over time.

CHARRED SHISHITO PEPPERS

If you see shishito peppers at the grocery store, grab them. They make for a quick and fun snack. Every one in ten is hot (or so they say)—which works well for families that like games and competition, like mine.

SERVES 2 TO 4

INGREDIENTS

12 shishito peppers	Flaked sea salt
1 Tbsp olive oil	

HOW TO

Preheat the barbecue to high heat. Brush the peppers with the olive oil. Grill them, turning occasionally, until charred, about 10 minutes. Alternatively, you can sauté these in a cast-iron pan, or grill pan over high heat on the stovetop. Remove from the heat and sprinkle with salt.

STUFFED + CHARRED JALAPENO PEPPERS

These are a perfect warm-weather snack if you're already at the barbecue. You can also make them a day ahead and grill when you're ready to serve. If you like heat, check page 42 to learn more about pepper heat.

SERVES 4

INGREDIENTS

Zest + juice of ½ lemon	3½ oz/100 g feta, crumbled
2 tsp olive oil	4 small jalapenos
1 tsp dried chopped thyme leaves	Flaked sea salt

HOW TO

In a small bowl, mix together the lemon zest and juice, olive oil, and thyme. Mix in the feta, and let marinate at room temperature for at least 30 minutes, or up to overnight in the fridge.

Preheat the barbecue to high heat. Use a paring knife, trim the stems, and remove the seeds from the cores of the jalapenos, but keep them whole so you can fill them with the feta. Remove the feta from the marinade and use a small spoon, or your hands, to stuff it into each jalapeno.

Grill the jalapenos, turning occasionally, until charred and the feta is softened and warm, about 10 minutes. Remove from the heat and sprinkle with salt.

COOK'S NOTE

For a creamier alternative, use a creamy goat cheese in place of the feta in the stuffed peppers. You can also swap small cubed cheese for crumbled.

PARMESAN + PANKO SNAP PEAS

These are a perfect snack to enjoy with drinks, especially served warm or at room temperature. I was inspired to create them by a recipe in one of my favourite, simple cookbooks, *The Forest Feast Gatherings* by Erin Gleeson.

SERVES 4

INGREDIENTS

4 cups stringless sugar snap peas, ends trimmed

1 Tbsp olive oil

⅓ cup grated Parmesan

⅓ cup panko breadcrumbs

¼ tsp cayenne pepper

1 sprig thyme, leaves only

Flaked sea salt + freshly cracked pepper

2 Tbsp salted pepitas

HOW TO

Preheat the oven to 400°F. Line a sheet pan with parchment paper. Arrange the snap peas in a single layer on the prepared pan and toss with the olive oil.

In a small bowl, combine the Parmesan, breadcrumbs, cayenne, thyme, and salt and pepper. Sprinkle on top of the snap peas.

Bake for 15 minutes or until the topping is golden brown. Remove from the oven and sprinkle with some more salt, and the pepitas. Serve warm or at room temperature.

THE SKINNY ON SNACKS

To keep an easy, healthy snack on hand at all times: After grocery shopping, clean and prep your vegetables before you put them away. Store them in stackable airtight containers in the fridge so they're ready to be eat (some vegetables, like carrots, are best stored in water). Sprinkle your vegetables (even cauliflower and broccoli stems) with a little salt to bring out their flavour. And take your vegetables one step further with the simple recipes in this chapter. Open-face toasts (page 51) have endless variations for vegetables; prepare a few days' worth. When the family is feeling peckish, steer them toward these easy-to-grab options and away from the dreaded snack cupboard.

RADISHES WITH FLAKED SALT

My grandmother used to eat raw radishes dipped in cold butter and salt. As a child, I thought this was an old lady thing. But when I was working in France in my twenties, I noticed they were as common on the table as bread. Then I saw them featured in cookbooks by both Julia Child and Alice Waters and I realized they're a classic. It wasn't until we planted our own radishes and watched them magically spring from the earth, that I grew to truly love and appreciate their simple yet powerful peppery-ness.

SERVES 4 TO 6

INGREDIENTS

2 bunches radishes, ends trimmed

1 Tbsp flaked sea salt

1 Tbsp butter, room temperature

HOW TO

Place the radishes in a pretty bowl. Add the salt and butter to separate little side dishes. Let everyone salt and butter to suit their own taste. In France (or at your grandmother's table), the butter would traditionally be served cold, but for ease, go ahead and use room-temperature butter—and surprise the family with the deliciousness of this simple snack.

SIMPLE TOASTS

Toasts: simple, classic, versatile, and just the perfect snack. They're my way of saying I love good bread, and also give you the perfect excuse to load up on toppings. Toasts look best served on rustic boards, which I collect from antique stores, old barns, and vintage shops. And a top tip if your house is on the market: pop a baguette into the oven just before an open house and the irresistible scent of warm bread will fill the air.

Following are recipes for three dips and seven toppings to spiff up toast with no fuss. They can all be made ahead of time and stored in an airtight container. And can be just as tasty as sides, on crackers, turned into salads, or paired with mains.

MAKES 12 TOASTS

INGREDIENTS

12 1-inch slices baguette
  (cut on a diagonal)

2 Tbsp olive oil

Flaked sea salt

Topping of your choice
  (pages 52 to 64)

HOW TO

Preheat the oven to 400°F. Place the baguette slices on a baking sheet and bake for about 7 minutes or until toasted, flipping partway through if you like. Remove from the oven, drizzle with the olive oil, and sprinkle with salt. Enjoy with the topping of your choice.

LEMON GOAT CHEESE

LIME CREMA

My friend Kara and I have been sharing food ideas for years. We were both cooks at tree-planting camps, and the experience taught us creativity, resilience, and how to cook for a large (and appreciative) crowd. She uses this recipe as a dip, but I love it on toast—and it's now one of my many simple and delicious go-to's.

Bent Taco in Collingwood makes the best fixings for the best tacos, like their lime crema. Crema is just a fancy word for adding acid and flavour to your sour cream. Here's my interpretation of their fancy-not-fancy crema. It's the perfect topping for tacos or a simple dip for vegetables or spread for toasts.

MAKES 12 TOASTS

MAKES 12 TOASTS

INGREDIENTS

1 (4 oz/113 g) small package goat cheese, softened

6 Tbsp plain yogurt

Zest + juice of ½ lemon

¼ cup dry-toasted pine nuts, or raw pepitas

2 tsp olive oil

Salt + freshly cracked pepper

1 recipe Simple Toasts (page 51)

INGREDIENTS

1 cup Greek yogurt or sour cream

2 cloves garlic, minced

2 green onions, white + light green parts only, sliced

Zest + juice of 1 lime

Salt + freshly cracked pepper

1 recipe Simple Toasts (page 51)

HOW TO

Mix together the cheese, yogurt, and lemon zest and juice. Transfer to a pretty, flat serving bowl and top with the nuts. Drizzle with the olive oil and season with salt and pepper. Serve alongside the toasts.

HOW TO

In a bowl, combine the yogurt, garlic, green onions, and lime zest and juice. Season with salt and pepper. Refrigerate, covered, for at least 30 minutes, or up to overnight. Serve alongside the toasts.

COOK'S NOTE

For how to dry-toast nuts see page 70.

COOK'S NOTE

Mexican crema is used in tacos and other spicy Mexican dishes to balance out their heat. You can use plain yogurt instead of Greek, and add a bit of salt and lemon juice in place of the lime, if you like.

ROASTED CAULIFLOWER + RICOTTA PUREE

This silky puree has a deep, roasted flavour. It can act as a dip for veggies or pita, as a side, or as a topper on toast, a baked potato, or anything grilled. It's the perfect light lunch or snack, and is hearty enough to almost make a meal of it. You can make it ahead of time and warm when you're ready to eat.

MAKES 12 TOASTS

INGREDIENTS

1 head cauliflower

2 cloves garlic, minced

2 Tbsp olive oil + extra for drizzling

Salt + freshly cracked pepper

⅓ cup ricotta

2 Tbsp tahini, or to taste

Pinch of cayenne, or to taste

Pinch of cumin, or to taste

2 Tbsp lemon juice

1 handful chopped flat-leaf parsley

1 recipe Simple Toasts (page 51)

HOW TO

Preheat the oven to 400°F. Discard the tough outer leaves and stem of the cauliflower. Break the remaining cauliflower into uniform florets. Rinse and pat dry.

Place the florets in a roasting dish, add the garlic and olive oil, and toss to combine. Season with salt and pepper. Roast for 20 minutes or until the florets are soft but al dente.

Transfer the florets to a food processor and add the ricotta, tahini, cayenne, cumin, and lemon juice, and puree until just smooth. Transfer to a serving bowl and top with chopped parsley and a drizzle of olive oil. Serve alongside the toasts.

COOK'S NOTE

For a chunkier texture, you can mash the florets with a potato masher.

SMOKED APPLEWOOD CHEDDAR + APPLE

Apple and cheddar on raisin walnut bread from ACE Bakery was one of my signature vegetarian sandwiches back in my dish café days. More than a decade on, I still love the combination—but now, open-faced.

MAKES 12 TOASTS

INGREDIENTS

2 small Granny Smith apples

Juice of 1 lemon

5 oz/140 g smoked Apple-
wood or aged cheddar

3 tsp honey

Salt + freshly cracked pepper

1 recipe Simple Toasts
(page 51)

HOW TO

Slice the apples lengthwise into 12 thin, ¼-inch-thick rounds, stopping way before the core. Brush with the lemon juice to avoid browning. Using a Y-peeler, knife, or cheese slicer, slice the cheese into 12 thin, ¼-inch-thick slices. Arrange the apple then the cheese on the toasts. Drizzle with the honey and season with salt and pepper.

COOK'S NOTE

When buying cheeses, always ask the pros behind the cheese counter for help. Cheese is an endless learning opportunity. (For example, don't be fooled into thinking the harder cheeses are lower in fat than the soft, creamy ones.) Serve cheese with your favourite jellies or condiments, like my red pepper jam from my second cookbook,
In My Mother's Kitchen.

SMOKED TROUT WITH CAPER CREAM CHEESE

I had the opportunity to visit Kolapore Springs—a hidden local and sustainable hatchery a stone's throw from my parents' farm—when I was working with Feast, a chef-driven food-delivery service in Toronto. Since tasting their trout I haven't turned back. It's a true fridge staple hero for a last-minute cocktail party. Kolapore Springs' trout is only sold locally, so use your favourite local smoked trout for this recipe.

MAKES 12 TOASTS

INGREDIENTS

Caper Cream Cheese:

Generous ½ cup cream cheese, softened

¼ cup capers, drained

¼ cup finely diced red onions

Zest + juice of ½ lemon

2 Tbsp chopped dill

Salt + freshly cracked pepper

1 recipe Simple Toasts (page 51)

1 side smoked trout, broken into large pieces

1 handful arugula microgreens

Zest of ½ lemon

HOW TO

For the caper cream cheese, in a bowl, combine the cream cheese, capers, onions, lemon zest and juice, dill, and salt and pepper. Generously and evenly spread over the toasts. Top each one with some smoked trout, a pinch of microgreens, and some lemon zest.

COOK'S NOTE

Sides of smoked trout vary in size. Use any leftovers in a salad, a sandwich, or pasta. The caper cream cheese is also delicious topped with minced jalapeno, and feel free to swap lime for the lemon. You can also add a thin slice of cucumber on top of the trout for a little crunch.

ROASTED TOMATOES + GOAT CHEESE

The classic combination of tomatoes and goat cheese is still one of my favourites (throw in some arugula and you have a salad for lunch). I like to serve these toasts family-style, with the toasts on one plate and the tomatoes and goat cheese in separate gratin dishes. Embrace the messiness.

MAKES 12 TOASTS

INGREDIENTS

1 pint cherry tomatoes

1 Tbsp olive oil

4 sprigs thyme, leaves only

Salt + freshly cracked pepper

1 tsp balsamic vinegar

1 (5 oz/140 g) package goat cheese, softened

1 recipe Simple Toasts (page 51)

Microgreens, for garnish

HOW TO

Preheat the oven to 450°F. Place the tomatoes in a small gratin dish or oval casserole. Drizzle with the olive oil, top with the thyme, and season with salt and pepper. Roast for 15 minutes or until the tomatoes start to pop and shrivel. Remove from the oven and drizzle with the balsamic. Generously spread the goat cheese on each toast, then spoon the tomatoes on top.

COOK'S NOTE

If you have a larger package of goat cheese, go ahead and use more if you like. Feel free to swap in feta for a saltier hit in place of the goat cheese and sprinkle with crushed pistachios for a crunch.

AVOCADO, ROASTED CORN + CHERRY TOMATOES

The oven-roasted corn in this recipe is a snack or a side dish in and of itself. Sometimes it gets polished off before it makes it onto the toast. The same goes for the oven-roasted tomatoes, another simple side dish. If you can resist eating them as you prep them, the corn and tomatoes are a winning combination with avocado on toast.

MAKES 12 TOASTS

INGREDIENTS

1 pint cherry tomatoes

2 Tbsp olive oil

3 sprigs thyme, leaves only

4 cobs corn, kernels cut off, or 1 cup frozen corn kernels, thawed

Salt + freshly cracked pepper

1 avocado

Zest + juice of 1 lime

1 tsp peperoncini piccanti or chili flakes, or to taste

1 recipe Simple Toasts (page 51)

HOW TO

Preheat the oven to 450°F. Line a sheet pan with parchment paper.

On one half of the prepared pan, scatter the tomatoes, drizzle with half of the olive oil, and top with the thyme. On the other half, place the corn kernels and drizzle with the remaining olive oil. Season everything with salt and pepper. Roast for about 15 minutes, or until the tomatoes pop and start to shrivel and the corn is golden.

In a bowl, use a fork to mash the avocado with the lime zest and juice. Stir in the peperoncini and season with more salt and pepper. Top the toasts with the smashed avocado, then the corn and tomatoes.

COOK'S NOTE

For an alternate, raw version of avocado toast, use raw sliced radishes in place of the corn and tomatoes.

HUMMUS, ROASTED RED PEPPER + ROASTED CORN

This is a perfect from-the-pantry snack that uses store-bought hummus. It calls for roasting a red bell pepper, but if you're looking for a quicker fix, feel free to use jarred roasted red peppers or sundried tomatoes instead.

MAKES 12 TOASTS

INGREDIENTS

1 red bell pepper

2 cobs corn, kernels cut off, or 1 cup frozen corn kernels, thawed

1 Tbsp olive oil

Salt + freshly cracked pepper

1 cup store-bought hummus

1 recipe Simple Toasts (page 51)

1 small handful baby arugula

HOW TO

Preheat the oven to 400°F. Line a sheet pan with aluminum foil.

If you have a gas burner, place the whole pepper directly into the high flame using metal tongs, turning to char it completely on all sides, about 6 minutes total. If you don't have a gas range, halve the pepper, discard the stem and seeds, and broil on a sheet pan until charred, about 5 minutes.

Seal the pepper in a plastic or paper bag and set aside to steam and cool. When cool enough to handle, remove from the bag and peel off the blackened skin (it should slide off easily). Don't rinse.

If you roasted the pepper on an open flame, discard the core and seeds. Slice the pepper into thin strips.

Place the corn on the prepared pan in a single layer. Drizzle with the olive oil, and season with salt and pepper. Roast for 15 minutes or until soft and golden.

To assemble, spread hummus on each toast. Top with some strips of pepper, a small handful of corn, and a pinch of baby arugula.

RICOTTA WITH FIGS + PISTACHIOS

In my first cookbook, *dish entertains*, the signature baked figs were a hit, and are to this day. This recipe is a nod to that rich, hot dish, but it's quicker to prepare and has the illusion of being lighter than the original. Toss with a base of microgreens and this becomes a beautiful salad.

MAKES 12 TOASTS

INGREDIENTS

Whipped Ricotta:

1 cup ricotta

Zest of 1 lemon

Juice of ½ lemon

3 sprigs thyme, leaves only

Salt + freshly cracked pepper

¼ cup pistachios, shelled + roughly chopped

2 Tbsp aged balsamic vinegar

6 fresh figs, quartered

2 Tbsp honey

1 recipe Simple Toasts (page 51)

HOW TO

For the whipped ricotta, in a stand mixer fitted with the paddle attachment or using a fork in a small bowl, mix together the ricotta, lemon zest and juice, thyme, and salt and pepper until fluffy and incorporated.

In a small fry pan over medium-high heat, dry-toast the pistachios, shaking frequently, until fragrant, about 2 minutes.

If your balsamic is runny, in a very small saucepan, boil it until thickened and set aside to cool.

Spread the ricotta on the toasts. Layer the figs on top, sprinkle with pistachios, and drizzle with the honey and balsamic.

COOK'S NOTE

To candy the pistachios, toast them per the recipe and set aside. In a small saucepan over medium heat, cook 1 to 2 tablespoons of honey or maple syrup, swirling the pan until it starts to caramelize. Stir in the nuts to coat and remove from the heat. Once cooled, break them apart. You can also try toasted or candied walnut pieces, or pepitas, in this recipe.

CREAMY FOREST MUSHROOMS

This topping is a rich, flavourful, and versatile combination. It's delicious on toast, but you can also ditch the bread and toss it with some cooked egg noodles instead for a quick dinner. Or add stock and turn it into mushroom soup. It could also become a tasty sauce for chicken.

MAKES 12 TOASTS

INGREDIENTS

2 Tbsp butter

¼ cup finely diced shallots

3 cups diced assorted mushrooms

2 sprigs thyme, leaves only

Pinch of cayenne, or to taste

¼ cup white wine

⅓ cup whipping cream

Salt + freshly cracked pepper

2 green onions, white + light green parts only, thinly sliced

3 Tbsp grated Parmesan (optional)

1 recipe Simple Toasts (page 51)

HOW TO

In a large skillet over medium heat, melt the butter. Add the shallots and sauté for a few minutes until softened. Add the mushrooms and thyme, and sauté for a few more minutes until no liquid remains. Add the cayenne and sauté for 30 seconds more. Increase the temperature to high. Deglaze the pan with the wine, scraping up any bits that have stuck to the bottom of the pan.

Add the cream and simmer, stirring until the mixture starts to thicken and coats the back of the spoon. Season with salt and pepper.

Top the toasts with the mushroom mixture, and garnish with green onions and Parmesan (if using).

Assorted mushrooms such as cremini, porcini, and/or button are great in this dish.
Feel free to just use one mushroom variety, though, if that's what you have.

SALADS

THE SKINNY ON SALADS

Salads are an everyday thing for me, and the perfect way to eat raw vegetables with little effort. Whether it's a simple green salad with your favourite balsamic vinaigrette, or a more elaborate creation, follow the seasons and make salads with what's available locally. And have fun with it. Experiment with the shapes and sizes of your colourful ingredients, and enjoy a combination of flavours and textures with cheeses, nuts, and seeds. Use pretty salad bowls and interesting serving utensils for a picture-worthy salad.

Whether I buy greens from the grocery store or the farmers' market, or I pull them fresh from the garden, I give the whole leaves a good wash as soon as I get home, and dry them thoroughly in the salad spinner. Once dry, wrap them in a tea towel and store them

in the crisper. Our family favourite lettuce is butter, also called Bibb.

I usually whisk dressing ingredients in a measuring cup and store leftovers in a mason jar on the counter for the next day. For a simple dressing, I'll free-pour equal parts olive oil and vinegar over the salad and toss to coat.

The salads in this book are best enjoyed the day they are made. Fresh is best. But the lettuce washing, vegetable prep, or nut or seed toasting can all be done ahead of time. I usually toss the salad with the dressing just before serving, unless the recipe calls for resting to let the flavours meld.

RAW SPRING SALAD

Every new season brings fresh flavours, and with change comes hope and optimism. When in season, there's nothing like the first taste of radishes, asparagus, and sugar snap peas. In this recipe, I serve them straight-up raw and in a variety of shapes for a pretty and elegant salad, ideal for entertaining.

SERVES 4

INGREDIENTS

Salad:

1 bunch asparagus, ends snapped off

1 bunch radishes, ends removed

½ cup sugar snap peas

1 handful pea shoots

1 handful microgreens

Vinaigrette:

3 Tbsp plain yogurt

3 Tbsp olive oil

2 Tbsp red wine vinegar

1 Tbsp maple syrup

Salt + freshly cracked pepper

Optional Toppings:

¼ cup pepitas

1 bunch chives, finely chopped

¼ cup crumbled goat cheese

HOW TO

For the salad, using a mandoline, chef's knife, or Y-peeler, thinly shave the asparagus, radishes, and snap peas lengthwise. Place the shavings in a pretty salad bowl.

For the vinaigrette, in a small bowl, whisk together the yogurt, olive oil, vinegar, and maple syrup. Season with salt and pepper.

To toast the pepitas, place in a small fry pan over medium heat and dry-toast, shaking frequently, until fragrant and light brown. Remove from the pan and sprinkle with salt.

When ready to serve, toss the vegetables and microgreens with the vinaigrette. Top with chives, toasted pepitas, and goat cheese.

GRILLED ROMAINE + FRIED CAPERS

This is a sexy Caesar stand-in people will notice. It eats like a meal—knife and fork required—but it's not the most elegant first-date material. Rough-chop it after you wow and dazzle your guests for ease of eating. The dressing also makes a great dip; it's perfect with celery, carrots, and radishes—step aside, hummus.

SERVES 4

INGREDIENTS

Salad:

2 romaine hearts

3 Tbsp avocado oil

½ cup capers, drained

Salt + freshly cracked pepper

4 radishes, thinly sliced

Creamy Vinaigrette:

4 to 6 Tbsp lemon juice

2 Tbsp tahini, or to taste

2 Tbsp avocado or olive oil

1 tsp Dijon mustard

3 tsp honey

Salt + freshly cracked pepper

HOW TO

Preheat the barbecue to high heat. Slice the romaine hearts in half lengthwise.

In a sauté pan over medium heat, warm 1 tablespoon of the avocado oil and fry the capers until they pop and are crisp, about 2 minutes. Set aside. Brush the remaining oil over the romaine (less is better, as romaine is like a sponge). Season with salt and pepper.

Grill the romaine cut-side down until charred and warmed through, about 6 to 8 minutes.

Flip and grill until the underside is charred and softened, about 5 minutes.

Meanwhile, for the vinaigrette, in a bowl, whisk together the lemon juice (start with 4 tablespoons and add more as required), tahini, oil, mustard, and honey. Season with salt and pepper and set aside.

Transfer the romaine to a platter and drizzle with as much dressing as you like. Top with the fried capers and the radishes.

RAW SHAVED SUMMER SALAD

This is a pretty salad for summer entertaining, and it's worth waiting for the season to get the best selection of the most delicious local ingredients you can find.

SERVES 4 TO 6

INGREDIENTS

Dressing:

3 Tbsp olive oil

2 Tbsp tahini

2 Tbsp lemon juice

1 clove garlic, minced

1 tsp honey

Salt + freshly cracked pepper

Salad:

4 stalks celery

3 carrots, peeled (yellow, orange + purple, if available)

3 beets, peeled (striped, yellow + red, if available)

1 yellow or green zucchini

1 generous handful arugula leaves or spring mix

¼ cup chopped chives

¼ cup chopped Italian parsley leaves

¼ cup chopped celery tops

HOW TO

For the dressing, in a small bowl, whisk together the olive oil, tahini, lemon juice, garlic, and honey. Season with salt and pepper. Set aside.

For the salad, using a mandoline, chef's knife, or Y-peeler, slice the celery, carrots, beets, and zucchini paper-thin. In a shallow salad bowl, layer the celery, carrots, zucchini, and beets on top or alongside of each other. Drizzle with the dressing.

Allow the vegetables to marinate in the fridge for at least 15 minutes before serving. Just before serving, add the arugula and herbs around the vegetables. Serve in this pretty presentation, and then toss after serving, if you like.

COOK'S NOTE

Use the summer herbs of your choice in place of some or all of the parsley. I love chervil, parsley's elegant cousin.

BEET + RHUBARB SALAD WITH PICKLED RED ONIONS

This is a special occasion salad. The beets require a little bit of work, but it's worth it, and you can double up so you have extras another day. You can make them ahead and assemble everything at the last minute—just wear gloves to avoid ruining your manicure.

SERVES 4 TO 6

INGREDIENTS

6 red beets, trimmed

½ red onion, thinly sliced

4 Tbsp sherry vinegar

2 Tbsp sugar

2 Tbsp maple syrup

4 to 6 stalks rhubarb, thickly sliced on the diagonal

2 cups watercress, stems trimmed

3 Tbsp olive oil

Salt + freshly cracked pepper

3½ oz/100 g Gorgonzola, cut into small chunks

HOW TO

In a large pot of water, add the beets, bring to a boil, and boil until just softened, about 30 minutes depending on their size. Set aside to cool enough to handle. Peel off and discard the skins. Cut the beets into wedges. Set aside.

While the beets are cooking, in a medium bowl, cover the onions with the vinegar, and refrigerate for 30 minutes.

In a large nonstick pan over medium heat, warm the sugar, stirring, until it melts. Watch it carefully so it doesn't burn. Stir in the maple

syrup and 2 tablespoons of water, and add the rhubarb. Cook until the rhubarb begins to soften but still maintains its colour, about 5 minutes. You don't want it to go mushy.

In a large, beautiful bowl, toss the watercress with enough olive oil to coat, and season with salt and pepper. Evenly layer the onions overtop and drizzle with half their pickling vinegar. Top with the rhubarb and cheese. Drizzle with more oil and pickling vinegar if needed.

COOK'S NOTE

*Feel free to swap out the Gorgonzola for your favourite blue cheese. Or skip
the cheese for a dairy-free version. If you already have Pickled Onions (page 40) in
your fridge, use those instead. Add large croutons at the end for more substance.*

SHAVED CELERIAC SALAD

Peter's dad was known in his house for this French-inspired salad delicacy. I never met him, but it's clear that Peter gets his salad-making interest from him. The star of this salad is the celeriac, also known as celery root—or the bulbous root you aren't sure what to do with when it comes in your produce delivery box. It's not the prettiest of vegetables, but it always turns into a refreshing and delicious salad. This salad is the perfect match with fish. If you have leftovers, make a quick vegetable stock. Try the Cream of Celery + Celeriac Soup too (page 112).

SERVES 4

INGREDIENTS

1 medium celeriac

4 stalks celery

⅓ cup olive oil

¼ cup Champagne or white wine vinegar

⅓ cup chopped chervil

Salt + freshly cracked pepper

¼ cup chopped hazelnuts, toasted (optional)

HOW TO

Use a chef's knife to trim the top and bottom of the celeriac and a paring knife or Y-peeler to peel the skin. Cut the celeriac into 6 pieces. Using a mandoline or chef's knife, slice each piece very thinly—you want shavings. Transfer to a bowl.

Trim and discard the ends of the celery stalks. Reserve the celery leaves. Slice the celery very thinly on the diagonal and add to the bowl with the celeriac.

In a measuring cup, whisk together the olive oil, vinegar, and half the chervil. Season with salt and pepper. Toss the celeriac and celery with the vinaigrette to coat.

Plate the salad on a pretty platter. Season with more salt and pepper and top with the remaining chervil and the hazelnuts (if using).

COOK'S NOTE

Shaved vegetables are prettiest for this dish, but you can also grate them to make it more like a slaw and easier to eat.

ROASTED CORN, AVOCADO + TOMATO SUCCOTASH

This is a classic summer combination, but don't let the seasonality stop you from enjoying it all year round. Cherry tomatoes seem to hold their flavour into the colder months. I love to buy local corn in season and freeze it so it's there when I want it. This salad can be made a day ahead, just add the avocado right before serving.

SERVES 4

INGREDIENTS

2 cobs corn or 2 cups frozen corn kernels, thawed

1 jalapeno, stem removed, deseeded + minced

¼ cup + 1 Tbsp olive oil

Salt + freshly cracked pepper

Zest + juice of 2 limes (about ¼ cup juice)

1 red bell pepper, diced

1 pint cherry tomatoes, halved

½ red onion, diced or sliced

½ of a (14 oz/400 g) round feta (sliced crosswise, to keep the circular shape)

1 avocado, diced

3 sprigs thyme, for garnish

HOW TO

Preheat the oven to 450°F. Line a sheet pan with parchment paper. If using fresh corn, remove the kernels from the cob.

Place the corn kernels onto the prepared pan. Scatter the jalapenos overtop, drizzle with 1 tablespoon of the olive oil, and season with salt and pepper. Roast the corn for 10 to 15 minutes or until softened and browned, stirring halfway through. Set aside to cool.

In a small bowl, whisk together the lime zest and juice with the remaining olive oil and season with salt and pepper.

In a bowl, combine the bell peppers, tomatoes, and onions with the roasted corn and jalapenos. Toss and coat with the lime vinaigrette. Chill the salad in the fridge for 1 hour.

To plate, place the feta in the centre of a serving plate and spoon the salad around it. Add the avocado and garnish thyme just before serving.

TOMATO, PEACH + BURRATA

Tomatoes are a fruit so pair naturally with their summer companion, peaches. Enjoy this salad with a glass of crisp cold Chablis (or lemonade) and imagine you're on the porch swing.

SERVES 4

INGREDIENTS

6 field tomatoes

Flaked sea salt + freshly cracked pepper

4 Tbsp olive oil

3 Tbsp aged balsamic vinegar

4 peaches

1 ball burrata

2 handfuls watercress microgreens

HOW TO

Slice the tomatoes and layer in a shallow serving bowl. Season with salt and pepper and drizzle with half the olive oil and balsamic to coat.

Cut the peaches in half, discard the pits, and cut into wedges lengthwise, keeping the skins on. Layer the peaches on top of the tomatoes.

Pull off large pieces of burrata and place on top of the peaches. Top with the microgreens. Drizzle with the remaining oil and vinegar and season with salt and pepper. Serve immediately.

CHERRIES + TOMATOES WITH BURRATA

This seasonal summer salad is as delicious as it is gorgeous. Get your phone out, as you'll want to take a photo…then devour it.

SERVES 4

INGREDIENTS

1 pint mixed yellow + red grape + cherry tomatoes, halved

1 cup fresh halved, pitted cherries

2 Tbsp aged balsamic vinegar

½ cup chiffonade basil + extra to garnish

1 ball burrata

1 Tbsp olive oil

Flaked sea salt

Simple Toasts (page 51)

HOW TO

In a bowl, toss the tomatoes and cherries with the balsamic. Let sit at room temperature for 15 minutes. Stir in the basil.

Place the whole burrata on a serving board, lightly drizzle with the olive oil, and sprinkle with salt. Spoon the tomato and cherry mixture over the whole burrata. Garnish with more basil.

Serve with toasts on the side. The first guest gets to break into the whole burrata and make a delicious mess.

COOK'S NOTE

If you're already at the barbecue, place bread directly on the grill for a few minutes on each side for a delicious smoky flavour.

SIMPLE LETTUCE SALAD

It may seem strange to share a recipe for a very basic green salad, but this book would feel incomplete without a nod to the essential green salad we eat most nights. Feel free to mix and match your favourite greens. Butter or Bibb (both names are used interchangeably) lettuce is usually my favourite, but the early spring leaves of buttercrunch and red leaf my dad grows in the greenhouse can't be beat.

SERVES 4

INGREDIENTS

Salad:

1 head Bibb lettuce, torn

1 head radicchio, leaves separated

3 green onions, white + light-green parts only, thinly sliced

Vinaigrette:

2 Tbsp aged balsamic vinegar

2 Tbsp olive oil

Salt + freshly cracked pepper

HOW TO

For the salad, in a shallow salad bowl, arrange both sets of leaves and the green onions.

For the vinaigrette, in a measuring cup, whisk together the vinegar and olive oil, and season with salt and pepper.

Just before serving, gently toss the salad with the vinaigrette.

TACO SLAW

This slaw is the perfect side. It can be served with tacos (page 192), ribs (pages 225 and 226), or any grilled dish. Charlotte loves this, so it comes kid approved.

SERVES 4 AS A SIDE SALAD

INGREDIENTS

Slaw:

½ cup thinly sliced red and/or green cabbage

½ cup thinly sliced kale

½ cup thinly sliced Brussels sprouts or broccoli florets

3 green onions, white + light green parts only, sliced

1 jalapeno, stem and seeds discarded, finely minced

Marinade:

Zest + juice of 2 limes

2 Tbsp olive oil

1 Tbsp celery seed

1 Tbsp sugar

Salt + freshly cracked pepper

HOW TO

For the slaw, in a large bowl, combine the cabbage, kale, Brussels sprouts, green onions, and jalapenos.

For the marinade, in a jar, combine the lime zest and juice, olive oil, celery seed, sugar, and salt and pepper. Shake well. The marinade can be made ahead and stored in an airtight jar in the fridge for up to 1 week.

Pour the marinade over the vegetables and use a fork to mix it through and coat. Chill in the fridge for at least 30 minutes, or up to 2 days.

COOK'S NOTE

You can use 1½ cups pre-mixed chopped slaw ingredients of your choice instead of doing all the chopping yourself. Or try a mix of ½ cup each of thinly sliced apple, cabbage, and radish as a fun alternative to the green onions and jalapeno.

MUSHROOM, PARMESAN + ARUGULA SALAD

This is a classic fall salad staple. But you can take it a step further by breading and frying your mushrooms in a bit of butter and serving this salad warm.

SERVES 4

INGREDIENTS

Vinaigrette:

Zest + juice of 1 lemon

½ shallot, finely diced

½ cup olive oil

1 tsp honey

Salad:

5 cups baby arugula, trimmed

8 oz/225 g cremini mushrooms, shaved

4 oz/113 g chunk Parmesan, shaved

HOW TO

For the vinaigrette, in a measuring cup, whisk together the lemon zest and juice, shallots, olive oil, and honey. Set aside.

For the salad, in a shallow serving bowl, toss together the arugula and vinaigrette to coat. Using a chef's knife, very thinly slice the mushrooms. Top the arugula with the mushrooms and sprinkle with the Parmesan.

COOK'S NOTE

King oyster mushrooms are a fun and delicious alternative to cremini.

PEAR + BIBB LETTUCE WITH PECANS + GORGONZOLA

You can't beat this delicious fall combination. It's like a cheese platter disguised as a salad. It's also great for entertaining.

SERVES 4 TO 6

INGREDIENTS

2 heads torn Bibb lettuce

2 Bartlett pears

¼ cup lemon juice

½ cup whole pecans

¼ cup salted pepitas

2 Tbsp honey

¼ cup olive oil

Salt + freshly cracked pepper

3 oz/85 g Gorgonzola

HOW TO

Place the lettuce leaves in a shallow serving bowl. Using a mandoline or chef's knife, thinly slice the pears (skin on with stem and seeds intact is prettier). Pour 1 tablespoon of the lemon juice over the pear slices. Set aside.

In a small fry pan over medium heat, fry the pecans and pepitas for a few minutes until fragrant. Add the honey and stir to coat. Keep stirring until the honey starts to harden and candies the nuts. Be careful not to burn.

In a measuring cup, whisk together the remaining lemon juice and the olive oil, and season with salt and pepper. Drizzle over the lettuce leaves.

To serve, arrange the pears in a fan over the lettuce and sprinkle with the nuts, seeds, and cheese.

COOK'S NOTE

You can add or swap out the seeds and nuts for your own favourites, or add or substitute dried fruits (cherries or cranberries) or fresh late fall/holiday fruits (like figs and pomegranate seeds).

VEGGIE-ISH COBB-ISH SALAD

This hearty chopped salad bowl is perfect for a standalone lunch and can be tweaked to suit your own tastes. You can eliminate the romaine (it's more authentic that way), add olives, or turn it into a dinner by adding protein, like chicken. Your salad, your choice.

SERVES 4 TO 6

INGREDIENTS

Salad:

1 head romaine, roughly chopped

1 English cucumber, skin on + cut into large dice

1 pint cherry tomatoes, halved

½ recipe Pickled Onions (page 40)

Vinaigrette:

3 Tbsp olive oil

3 Tbsp plain Greek yogurt

Zest + juice of 1 lemon (about ¼ cup juice)

1 clove garlic, minced

1 tsp chopped oregano leaves

Salt + freshly cracked pepper

Toppings:

4 hardboiled eggs, quartered

1 avocado, cubed (optional)

½ cup cubed feta

HOW TO

For the salad, in a large bowl, combine the romaine, cucumbers, tomatoes, and pickled onions.

For the vinaigrette, in a bowl, whisk together the olive oil, yogurt, lemon zest and juice, garlic, and oregano, and season with salt and pepper.

Pour the dressing over the salad and toss to coat. Transfer to a pretty serving bowl. Top with the eggs, avocados (if using), and feta.

APPLE + BABY SPINACH SALAD

An oldie but a goodie. Even my kids love spinach this way.

SERVES 4 TO 6

INGREDIENTS

Apple Cider Vinaigrette:

¼ cup apple cider vinegar

2 Tbsp lemon juice

1 Tbsp maple syrup or honey

1 clove garlic, minced

⅓ cup olive oil

Salad:

6 to 8 cups baby spinach or mixed greens

2 large Pink Lady apples, skin on, cut into matchsticks

¼ small red onion, thinly sliced

½ cup walnut or pecan halves, toasted

¾ cup cranberries

1 small (4 oz/113 g) package goat cheese, crumbled

HOW TO

For the vinaigrette, in a small bowl, whisk together the vinegar, lemon juice, maple syrup, and garlic. Slowly whisk in the olive oil in a steady stream. Set aside.

For the salad, in a large salad bowl, toss the spinach with the vinaigrette to coat. Top with the apples, onions, nuts, cranberries, and cheese.

COOK'S NOTE

You can replace half or all of the baby spinach with kale, and swap out the goat cheese for feta, and the cranberries for dried cherries or blueberries. A whole new salad. My dad makes his own apple cider vinegar, but you can look for apple cider vinegar at farmers' markets or use small-producer vinegars.

CHRISTMAS EUCHRE TOURNEY SALAD

Our friends in Creemore host a big annual euchre tournament. The first year I was invited, I was new to euchre—which was not going to work for this party. So I won them over by offering to bring a salad, which became a ritual. Years later, I tied for second place and won part of the pot of money. Even so, I'm still terrible at euchre. But it's one of the best nights—all about friends, good food, and games.

SERVES 6

INGREDIENTS

3 cups peeled, deseeded + cubed butternut squash

¼ cup + 1 Tbsp olive oil

Salt + freshly cracked pepper

1 red bell pepper

4 cups chopped kale + mixed greens

¼ cup aged balsamic vinegar

1½ cups Pickled Onions (page 40)

¼ cup pepitas, toasted

½ cup soft goat cheese

HOW TO

Preheat the oven to 425°F. Line a baking sheet with aluminum foil. Spread the squash out on the prepared sheet. Drizzle with 1 tablespoon of the olive oil and season with salt and pepper. Bake for 30 minutes or until the squash is soft and brown. Set aside to cool.

If you have a gas burner, place the whole pepper directly into the high flame using metal tongs, turning to char it completely on all sides, about 6 minutes total. If you don't have a gas range, halve the pepper, discard the stem and seeds, and broil on a sheet pan until charred, about 5 minutes.

Seal the pepper in a plastic or paper bag and set aside to steam and cool. When cool enough to handle, remove from the bag and peel off the blackened skin (it should slide off easily). Don't rinse. If you roasted the pepper on an open flame, discard the core and seeds. Slice the pepper into thin strips.

To assemble the salad, combine the kale, remaining olive oil, and the balsamic. Season with salt and pepper, and toss to coat. Layer the squash, bell peppers, pickled onions, pepitas, and goat cheese on top.

COOK'S NOTES

*To save time, use frozen, chopped squash and bake from frozen. Consider roasting a few
extra red bell peppers and storing them in an airtight container to use in salads another day.
They'll keep refrigerated for up to 4 days. Or use a small jar of roasted red peppers instead.*

NEW YEAR'S EVE CATCH-ALL SALAD

For the past many years, we've had New Year's Eve hosted by our friends Tori and Cam, along with other great friends going back to our high school and university days. Some years there are bonfires or a nighttime cross-country ski by headlamp. But every year there is drinking, eating, and laughter. Mark and Heidi bring the oysters and steaks, Rahat and Mouse and Kate and Dan bring appies and breakfast for the next day, while Cam bartends and mans the firepit and barbecue and Tori sets the mood as the host-with-the-most and DJ. We bring our salad and "very expensive" wine. The salad ends up being a catch-all of whatever is left in the fridge post-Christmas; this version was worth jotting down.

SERVES 6 TO 8

INGREDIENTS

½ red onion, sliced

Juice of 2 limes

4 carrots, peeled + grated

¼ cup olive oil

¼ cup aged balsamic vinegar

1 tsp Dijon mustard

1 tsp honey

Salt + freshly cracked pepper

4 cups baby arugula

4 cups baby spinach

4 oz/113 g goat cheese, crumbled

6 figs, halved (optional)

½ cup shelled pistachios (optional)

HOW TO

In a small bowl, place the onions and cover with the juice of 1 lime. In another small bowl, place the carrots and cover with the juice of the other lime. Chill both in the fridge for about 30 minutes.

In a measuring cup, whisk together the olive oil, balsamic, mustard, and honey, and season with salt and pepper.

To assemble, mix the salad greens in a shallow salad bowl. Toss with the vinaigrette to coat. Arrange the marinated onions and carrots overtop. Sprinkle with the goat cheese, figs (if using), and pistachios (if using).

SOUPS

In my grandmother's kitchen, there was very little waste. She gave careful consideration to all her meals. Soups were a mainstay for her as they use up leftover vegetables, have the best homemade flavour, and they are easy on the wallet and comfort food for the belly.

I use the terms "stock" and "broth" interchangeably, but to be accurate: stocks tend to be thicker and made with bones, and broths are slightly thinner and made with herbs and vegetables. For the recipes in this book,

I usually use store-bought chicken "broth" for its convenience—but use what you want for your soups. Flavourful stocks and broths are available to buy from the butcher, off the shelf, or of course you can make your own like my grandmother did.

All vegetables make great soup. Whether you use classic soup mirepoix vegetables, like celery, carrots, and onions, or less common ones like celeriac (page 112) or asparagus, you can turn almost all of them into a delicious

soup. Try using a classic bouquet garni of bay leaf, parsley stems, and peppercorns, or flavour to your own taste. And if you want something more substantial than a vegetable soup, simply add a protein of your choice.

If someone in your house has dietary restrictions, skip the dairy used in a soup entirely or use plant-based dairy alternatives. And you can use oil in place of butter.

I find the debate with soups is whether to make them smooth or chunky. If you want a well-blended soup, use an immersion blender for a quick puree (or transfer the soup to a blender once it has cooled). If you prefer your soup chunky, only partly puree.

When you're going to make soup, consider doubling up the recipe. Let the soup cool completely before storing to prevent bacteria from growing. Then either refrigerate in mason jars for up to 2 days, or freeze in stackable airtight containers.

ROASTED TOMATO + RED PEPPER SOUP

It's hard to beat the depth of flavour and sweetness you get from roasting tomatoes, but if it's too hot to turn on the oven, a quick and simple sauté makes for a summer soup that is just as refreshing and delicious. Come winter, don't shy away from using cans of San Marzanos or look for fire-roasted tomatoes for maximum flavour.

SERVES 6

INGREDIENTS

2 lb/900 g Roma tomatoes, cut into thirds, or 2 (28 oz/ 796 ml each) cans San Marzano tomatoes with juices

1 red bell pepper, cut into large chunks

3 Tbsp olive oil

1 Tbsp sugar

Salt + freshly cracked pepper

3 Tbsp aged balsamic vinegar

2 Tbsp butter

1 large sweet onion, chopped

4 cups chicken stock

½ cup chopped basil

HOW TO

Preheat the oven to 450°F. Line a sheet pan with parchment paper. Arrange the tomatoes and peppers in a single layer on the prepared pan, drizzle with the olive oil, sprinkle with the sugar, and season with salt and pepper. Toss to coat. Roast for 20 minutes. Drizzle with the balsamic and roast for another 10 minutes until the tomatoes are softened and caramelized.

In a large, heavy-bottomed stockpot over medium heat, melt the butter. Add the onions and sauté for 10 minutes or until the onions are softened and light brown. Season with salt and pepper. Add the tomatoes and peppers, and sauté for 5 minutes. Add the stock and bring to a boil. Lower the heat and simmer until the vegetables are tender, about 10 minutes. Remove from the heat.

Using an immersion blender (or a blender, working in batches), puree until smooth.

To serve, ladle the soup into soup bowls, finish with basil, and season with salt and pepper.

TOMATO BASIL SOUP WITH FRIED CHICKPEAS

This quick summer soup, simply made from pantry items, is packed with subtle, smoky spices. The added protein helps to fill the belly.

SERVES 6

INGREDIENTS

3 Tbsp butter

1 large onion, chopped

1 medium carrot, grated

3 tsp harissa or 1 tsp chili flakes, or to taste

1¼ tsp cumin, or to taste

4 to 5 large ripe field tomatoes, peeled + cut into chunks (about 4 cups)

1 (28 oz/796 ml) can San Marzano tomatoes

1 Tbsp sugar

3 cups chicken stock

Salt + freshly cracked pepper

½ cup packed basil leaves, chiffonade + extra to garnish

2 Tbsp vegetable oil

¼ tsp cayenne, or to taste

1 (14 oz/398 ml) can chickpeas, rinsed + patted dry

HOW TO

In a large, heavy-bottomed stockpot over medium heat, melt the butter. Add the onions and carrots, and sauté, stirring, until the onions soften, about 5 minutes. Add the harissa and 1 teaspoon of the cumin and fry for about 1 minute. Add the fresh tomatoes and sauté about 10 minutes or until slightly thickened. Stir in the canned tomatoes, sugar, and stock, and season with salt and pepper.

Bring the mixture to a boil, stirring constantly. Lower the heat to medium-low, cover, and simmer for about 10 minutes until cooked through. Remove from the heat and stir in half the basil. Set aside.

In a medium fry pan over medium-high heat, heat the vegetable oil. Add the remaining cumin and the cayenne, if using, and fry for 1 minute. Add the chickpeas and fry for about 10 minutes, shaking the pan, until light brown and some of them have split.

To serve, ladle the soup into soup bowls and top with the fried chickpeas and remaining basil.

COOK'S NOTE

*Harissa is a smoky, spicy Tunisian condiment made from hot chili pepper paste.
If you like heat, this is a good one to keep in your pantry for a garlicky, smoky addition. It
is great as a rub for grilled meats or grilled vegetables, or as a condiment for
burgers, an omelette or baked eggs, or fried rice.*

SIMPLE CARROT SOUP

Carrot soup was a staple in our home when I was growing up, and today my kids love to eat it too. It's evolved over the years. In my first cookbook it was basic, in my second it was more dressed up, and now it's modern-retro (with the old-school can of evaporated milk). Simple is best.

SERVES 6

INGREDIENTS

1 Tbsp butter

1 Tbsp olive oil

1 medium sweet Vidalia onion, chopped

2 lb/900 g carrots, peeled + chopped

5 cups chicken stock

1 (12 oz/354 ml) can evaporated milk

Salt + freshly cracked pepper

1 Tbsp chopped curly parsley

HOW TO

In a large, heavy-bottomed stockpot over medium heat, melt the butter and heat the olive oil. Add the onions and sauté until just soft. Add the carrots and sauté for about 5 minutes until they start to soften. Add the stock and bring to a boil. Reduce the heat to medium-low and simmer, covered, for about 20 minutes until the carrots are tender. Remove from the heat.

Using an immersion blender (or working in batches in a blender), puree until smooth. Stir in the evaporated milk.

To serve, gently warm the soup and ladle into soup bowls, season with salt and pepper, and top with the parsley.

COOK'S NOTE

You can go richer with this soup by using cream instead of evaporated milk. Or eliminate the dairy altogether and add another cup of stock. For a mildly spicy variation, fry 2 teaspoons of curry powder with the carrots.

HEARTY CORN CHOWDER

This chunky hot pot is a delicious all-in-one meal. With a creamy base, this isn't a light soup, but it's a crowd favourite. It's the perfect summer soup if you have leftover corn to use up. But don't shy away from making it in the winter, as frozen corn makes it quicker to whip up.

SERVES 6

INGREDIENTS

4 to 5 cobs corn

4 cups chicken stock

1 cup milk

1 cup whipping cream

4 slices bacon, chopped

1 large onion, finely diced

3 stalks celery, finely diced

1 large carrot, cut into small dice

1 lb/455 g baby red potatoes, skins on + halved

¼ tsp cayenne pepper, or to taste

Salt + freshly cracked pepper

2 Tbsp chopped chives, for garnish

HOW TO

Cut the kernels off the cobs and set aside for the chowder. In a large, heavy-bottomed stockpot, bring the bare corn cobs, stock, milk, and cream to a boil. Turn down the heat to medium-low and simmer, uncovered, for 20 minutes or until slightly thickened. Using tongs, remove the cobs from the cooking liquid and discard.

Meanwhile, in a 5-quart Dutch oven over medium-high heat, cook the bacon, stirring occasionally, until crispy and browned. Using a slotted spoon, transfer the bacon to a bowl and set aside.

In the same Dutch oven, over medium heat, add the onions, celery, and carrots and cook, stirring occasionally, until the onions are soft, about 7 minutes. Add the potatoes, corn kernels, and cayenne. Season with salt and pepper. Add the corn stock and bring the mixture to a light boil. Turn down the heat to simmer until the potatoes are tender, 10 to 15 minutes. Season with salt and pepper.

To serve, ladle the soup into soup bowls and garnish with the reserved bacon and the chives.

COOK'S NOTE

Go ahead and use frozen corn when fresh is not in season; skip the first step of boiling the cobs and simply combine the liquids to make the stock.

There are lots of variations possible with this soup: To add heat, add 1 diced jalapeno or fry 2 teaspoons curry powder at the start. To give it more colour, add 1 cup diced red bell pepper or a pint of halved grape tomatoes with the potatoes and corn kernels. To turn it into a meal, add 1 cup diced chorizo sausage and chicken with the potatoes and corn. To add some greens, add 1 cup spinach in the last 2 minutes.

For a creamier soup, you have 2 options: Transfer one-quarter of the soup to a blender, blend with an immersion blender until smooth, then stir it back into the rest of your chowder; or add 1 (14 oz/398 ml) can of creamed corn and don't bother with any blending.

CREAM OF CELERY + CELERIAC SOUP

My favourite soup when I was growing up was Campbell's cream of celery. I've evolved to making my own soups, but if you peek in my cupboard you'll still find some Campbell's on the shelves. This recipe is my take on my beloved canned classic. Kids will love it too.

SERVES 6

INGREDIENTS

3 Tbsp butter

½ sweet onion, chopped

1 large celeriac, peeled + chopped

1 lb/455 g celery stalk, chopped (leaves reserved, for garnish)

6 cups chicken stock

½ cup plain yogurt (optional)

2 Tbsp honey

Salt + freshly cracked pepper

HOW TO

In a large, heavy-bottomed stockpot over medium-high heat, melt the butter, but don't allow it to change colour. Add the onions and sauté until soft, about 3 minutes. Add the celeriac and celery, and sauté until they start to soften, about 3 minutes.

Stir in the stock, turn down the heat to medium, and simmer until tender, about 20 minutes. Remove from the heat.

Using an immersion blender (or working in batches in a blender), puree the soup until smooth. Add the yogurt and honey right at the end and give everything a quick blast just to combine thoroughly.

To serve, ladle the soup into soup bowls and garnish with the reserved celery leaves.

CREAMY LEEK + POTATO SOUP

This is a twist on Peter's family's favourite soup when he was growing up. I couldn't resist adding cooked celery to enrich this classic soup with its sweetness.

SERVES 6

INGREDIENTS

¼ cup butter

3 leeks, white parts only, chopped

1 medium onion, peeled + chopped

3 stalks celery, sliced

5 medium yellow-skinned potatoes, peeled + chopped

5 sprigs thyme, leaves only

Salt + freshly cracked pepper

4 cups chicken stock

¾ cup milk (optional)

2 oz/55 g Roquefort, crumbled (optional)

1 bunch green onions, white + light green parts only, sliced

HOW TO

In a large, heavy-bottomed stockpot over medium heat, melt the butter. Add the leeks, onions, and celery, and sauté just until the onions begin to soften, about 5 minutes. Add the potatoes and thyme, season with salt and pepper, and sauté for another 2 to 3 minutes, stirring constantly so that everything is well combined.

Stir in the stock. Bring to a boil, then turn down the heat to medium-low, cover, and simmer, stirring occasionally, until the potatoes are just tender, about 15 to 20 minutes. Remove from the heat.

Using an immersion blender (or working in batches in a blender), puree until partially chunky. Stir in the milk, if using. Reheat the soup over low heat as needed before serving, but do not let it come to a boil.

To serve, ladle the soup into soup bowls, sprinkle with the cheese (if using), and garnish with the green onions.

COOK'S NOTE

This soup is just as delicious if you eliminate the milk and cheese and use olive oil in place of butter to make it dairy-free. To make it vegan, use vegetable stock in place of chicken.

FOREST MUSHROOM SOUP

Mushroom soup is a favourite order of ours at restaurants. But you too can pull off a restaurant-style multilayered soup with this easy recipe. It calls for an assortment of mushrooms; I like the depth of flavour found in porcinis, but use whatever mix is your favourite.

SERVES 6

INGREDIENTS

2 Tbsp butter

1 Tbsp olive oil

1 shallot, finely diced

½ sweet onion, diced

2 lb/900 g assorted mushrooms, diced (porcini, cremini, button)

2 sprigs thyme, leaves only

1 tsp chopped tarragon leaves (optional)

¼ cup white wine

⅓ cup whipping cream

5 cups chicken stock (or stock of your choice)

Salt + freshly cracked pepper

¼ cup finely chopped flat-leaf parsley or chives

Crusty bread, for serving

HOW TO

In a large, heavy-bottomed stockpot over medium heat, melt the butter and warm the olive oil. Add the shallots and onions and sauté until softened, about 5 minutes. Add the mushrooms, thyme, and tarragon, and sauté a few minutes until the mushrooms have softened and the herbs are fragrant.

Increase the heat to high. Deglaze the pan with the wine, scraping up any bits that have stuck to the bottom of the pan and incorporating them. Stir in the cream and, while stirring, bring the mixture to a boil. Continue boiling until the mixture slightly reduces and thickens. Stir in the stock. Turn down the heat to medium and simmer, uncovered, until the mushrooms are softened and the mixture has thickened, about 15 minutes.

To serve, ladle the soup into soup bowls, season with salt and pepper, and finish with the parsley. Enjoy with crusty bread on the side.

COOK'S NOTE

*Dried mushrooms are a great pantry staple. You can add some to this soup,
or to Creamy Forest Mushrooms for a toast topping (page 64). To hydrate them,
simply reconstitute them in boiling water. If you want a silkier texture
for this soup, you can puree it.*

AUNT NANCY'S CARAMELIZED ONION SOUP

My aunt Nancy is a really good cook. It comes from years of major training from my grandmother and an appreciation for the little things like warming your soup bowls and chilling your salad plates, being patient with low and slow ribs, or standing over the gravy, stirring until it's perfect. This soup reflects her love and attention to the things that matter. She doesn't like battling the cheese on top of traditional onion soup (I don't suggest it on a first date) and so it goes on the bottom. Brilliant. You'll need onion soup bowls, 4-inch ramekins, or other ovenproof bowls for this recipe. This is a Christmas Eve tradition in our house.

SERVES 4

INGREDIENTS

1 Tbsp olive oil

3 large Spanish (or other sweet) onions, halved, peeled, thinly sliced + skins reserved

Salt + freshly cracked pepper

2 dried bay leaves

2 tsp Worcestershire

2 boxes (32 oz/900 ml each) beef stock

½ cup grated Gruyère

1 batch Simple Toasts (page 51), for serving

HOW TO

In a large, heavy-bottomed stockpot over medium heat, warm the olive oil. Add the onions and sauté until soft and lightly caramelized, about 15 minutes. Generously season with salt and pepper.

Add the bay leaves and then the Worcestershire to deglaze the pan, scraping up any bits that have stuck to the bottom of the pan and incorporating all the ingredients. Stir in the stock and several large pieces of onion skin. Turn down the heat to low and cook, covered, for about 1 hour or more until the onions reduce to a jammy consistency—they caramelize and sweeten the longer they cook. Discard the onion skins and bay leaves.

Preheat the oven to 300°F. Evenly divide the cheese among the bowls. Place the bowls on a sheet pan and warm them in the oven for a few minutes until the cheese melts.

To serve, ladle the hot soup into the warmed bowls. Season with salt and pepper and serve with toast on the side, and a sprinkling of cheese on top if you like.

COOK'S NOTE

*When you're picking onions, look for ones with firm, dark skins to give the soup
more flavour and colour, and store them in a cool, dark place. Keep the skins as
intact as possible when you remove them. This soup is even better when you reheat
it on the second day. Feel free to add more cheese to your leftovers.*

BUTTERNUT SQUASH MISO SOUP

A food indulgence of mine is stopping at Nutbar, a small Toronto healthy food haunt loved and adored for its soups and toasts. When I'm sick or run down, I crave their Harvest Miso Soup. There's something magical and healing in it. This is my take on that soup, and a nod to Kate, the owner, and her healthy food brand.

SERVES 6

INGREDIENTS

2 Tbsp coconut oil

1 tsp ground turmeric (optional)

1 medium sweet onion, cut into small dice

2 carrots, peeled + cut into small dice

2 cloves garlic, minced

3 to 4 cups peeled, cubed butternut squash (about one 2 lb/900 g squash)

2 Tbsp miso paste

Salt + freshly cracked pepper

4 to 5 cups chicken or vegetable stock

1 Tbsp minced ginger

¼ cup pepitas

1 cup chunky croutons (homemade or store-bought)

2 Tbsp chopped chives

HOW TO

In a large, heavy-bottomed stockpot over medium heat, warm the coconut oil. Fry the turmeric (if using) for 30 seconds. Add the onions and sauté until soft. Add the garlic and sauté until light brown and soft, about 2 to 3 minutes. Add the squash and sauté for 3 to 4 minutes to brown and soften. Add the miso and season with salt and pepper.

Stir in the stock and bring the mixture to a boil. Turn down the heat to medium-low, stir in the ginger, and simmer, covered, until the squash is tender, about 15 minutes.

Using an immersion blender (or working in batches in a blender), puree until smooth.

To serve, ladle the soup into soup bowls and top with pepitas, croutons and chives.

COOK'S NOTE

This is great with sweet potato in place of the squash, or try using half of each.
For added richness, you can add 1 (14 oz/398 ml) can of coconut milk before blending.

Miso paste is fermented soybean, a salty staple in Japanese cooking that is said to be good
for gut health. Use it with honey and soy sauce to make a sticky glaze for salmon (page 203)
or ribs (page 225). To make croutons quickly, just break Simple Toasts (page 51) into cubes.

MOM'S SIMPLE SWEET POTATO SOUP

This soup is an inexpensive, easy, and delicious way to eat sweet potato and reap all the benefits of the protein and vitamins. This soup and sweet potato fries, of course.

SERVES 6

INGREDIENTS

1 Tbsp olive oil

1 Tbsp butter

1 medium sweet onion, cut into small dice

2 cloves garlic, minced

3 to 4 medium sweet potatoes, peeled + cut into small dice (about 3 cups)

2 sprigs thyme, leaves removed + chopped

Salt + freshly cracked pepper

5 cups chicken stock

2 green onions, white + light green parts only, sliced lengthwise

HOW TO

In a large, heavy-bottomed stockpot over medium heat, warm the olive oil and melt the butter. Add the onions and sauté until soft. Add the garlic, and sauté until light brown and soft, about 2 to 3 minutes. Add the sweet potatoes and thyme. Sauté for 3 minutes to brown and soften. Season with salt and pepper.

Stir in the stock and bring the mixture to a boil. Turn down the heat to medium-low and simmer, covered, until the sweet potatoes are tender, about 15 minutes. Using an immersion blender (or working in batches in a blender), puree until smooth. Season with more salt and pepper.

To serve, ladle the soup into soup bowls and top each with some green onions.

COOK'S NOTE

For a smoky heat, add 1 finely chopped chipotle in adobo to the sautéed garlic and sauté for a minute or two before adding the sweet potato.

THAI-INSPIRED CHICKEN, COCONUT + LIME SOUP

When I was consulting for Mama Earth, a local organic food-delivery company, we worked hard to develop the prepared foods side of their business. We had fun coming up with the recipe names, which naturally poured out of the kitchen. This is my version of Chef Kurt's Lime in the Coconut.

SERVES 6

INGREDIENTS

1 Tbsp coconut oil

3 to 4 tsp green curry paste

1 jalapeno, minced

1 Tbsp grated ginger

1 red bell pepper, diced

6 boneless, skinless chicken thighs, cut into small chunks

Salt + freshly cracked pepper

4 cups chicken stock

1 (14 oz/398 ml) can coconut milk

1 cup green beans, cut into thirds

2 green onions, white and light green parts only, sliced

Zest + juice of 2 limes

HOW TO

In a large, heavy-bottomed stockpot over medium heat, melt the coconut oil. Add the curry paste, jalapeno, and ginger and fry, stirring constantly, until fragrant, about 2 minutes. Be careful, it sputters. Add the bell peppers and sauté until combined. Add the chicken, season with salt and pepper, and cook until browned, about 3 to 5 minutes.

Stir in the stock and coconut milk, and bring to a boil. After a few minutes, add the green beans. Turn down the heat to medium-low and simmer until the chicken is cooked and the beans are still a vibrant green, about 7 to 10 minutes.

To serve, ladle the soup into soup bowls, and top each with green onions, lime zest, and a few squirts of lime juice.

COOK'S NOTE

This is a great soup base that you can adapt to your liking: Bulk it up by adding half a 9 oz/250 g package rice vermicelli in the last 5 minutes (just after you've brought it to a simmer); for a more mellow heat, swap the green curry paste with red curry paste; make it with 2 lb/900 g shrimp in place of chicken and reduce the simmering time to about 3 minutes.

SIDES

THE SKINNY ON SIDES

Sides are the secret weapon to a successful and delicious meal. When I can, I make dinner out of a bunch of sides. The secret to the most delicious side is to use vegetables that are local and in season. Simply prepare them with butter or olive oil, salt, and pepper.

When you cook your vegetables, it's helpful to remember the garden. In the winter months, deep-from-the-earth root vegetables, like beets and potatoes, are boiled starting in cold water to slowly release the starch, and are also delicious roasted in the oven. In the summer, green above-ground vegetables, like peas and beans, can be placed into already boiling water for a quicker cook and to preserve their colour and nutrients. Spring vegetables, like asparagus, are so delicious they need little more than a flash blanch just until they soften. Or they can be prepared quickly on the grill or sautéed in a pan. Whatever the season, there is nothing like a fresh, simple, uncomplicated side.

SPRING SAUTÉ OF
SNAP PEAS + RADISHES

Oh, hello, spring sauté. Aren't you a pretty pan of crunchy pink and green.

SERVES 2 TO 4

INGREDIENTS

2 Tbsp butter

1 shallot, minced

1 (8 oz/225 g) package sugar snap peas

1 bunch radishes, quartered

Salt + freshly cracked pepper

½ bunch green onions, white + light green parts only, sliced diagonally

Zest of 1 lemon

1 tsp poppy seeds (optional)

HOW TO

In a large sauté pan over medium-high heat, melt the butter. Add the shallots and sauté until softened, about 2 minutes.

Add the snap peas and radishes, and season with salt and pepper. Continue to sauté for 3 to 5 minutes until the snap peas and radishes are just softened but vibrant in colour.

Add the green onions, lemon zest, and poppy seeds (if using). Season with salt and pepper and serve.

COOK'S NOTE

In spring, I add 1 bunch of asparagus (tips and stems) or about 1 cup fresh peas (blanched for 30 seconds) along with the sugar snap peas and radishes, or a pint of cherry tomatoes, halved in the summer. In the fall, add 1 cup sliced cremini mushrooms after sautéing the shallots to replace the radishes and snap peas. For additional flavour in any season, fry 1 teaspoon of mustard seeds in the butter before adding the shallots.

GRILLED SNAP PEAS, ASPARAGUS + GREEN ONIONS

Grilled green onions are delicious, and an overlooked vegetable to grill. They are the perfect side to steak (page 230) or a star ingredient in a grilled salad. Cook asparagus and green onions right on the grill and grill the sugar snap peas in a vegetable grill basket. Let the resident grill expert do the work.

SERVES 4

INGREDIENTS

1 cup sugar snap peas

1 large bunch green onions, white + light green parts only

1 bunch asparagus, ends removed

1 Tbsp olive oil

Salt + freshly cracked pepper

Vinaigrette:

¼ cup sour cream

3 Tbsp olive oil

2 Tbsp lemon juice

1 Tbsp tahini

2 tsp Dijon mustard

Salt + freshly cracked pepper

2 handfuls pea shoots

½ cup salted shelled pistachios, for garnish

HOW TO

Preheat the barbecue to medium heat. Place the snap peas, green onions, and asparagus on a platter, keeping them separate from each other. Drizzle with the olive oil and season with salt and pepper.

Place the snap peas in a grill basket and grill for about 5 minutes, shaking occasionally, until the snap peas are softened but still have some colour. Place the green onions and asparagus directly on the grill, setting them perpendicular to the grates so they don't fall through. Grill, turning the green onions and

asparagus occasionally, until charred and tender, about 5 minutes. Transfer to a large serving bowl.

For the vinaigrette, in a small bowl, whisk together the sour cream, olive oil, lemon juice, tahini, mustard, and salt and pepper.

In a medium bowl, toss the pea shoots with half of the vinaigrette. Drizzle the rest of the vinaigrette over the warm grilled vegetables. Place the pea shoots on top of the grilled vegetables and garnish with the pistachios.

COOK'S NOTE

*This side dish becomes a perfect meal with a couple of
fried eggs on top. If you skip the pea shoots, you have a grilled version
of a crudité, perfect to eat with your fingers and your favourite dip.*

ROASTED LEEKS WITH BROWN BUTTER

Leeks are a sign of spring. But wild leeks, referred to interchangeably as ramps, are the official sign of the start of the new season for chefs and local food movements. Wild leeks (pictured opposite) have a stronger, more pungent taste than the leeks you find at the grocery store year-round. They taste too intense raw, but they're delicious roasted or grilled. In my parents' maple syrup bush, around maple syrup season each April, they magically spring up as one of the earliest wild edibles, and we seize the moment to harvest as many as possible. Chefs freak out over them because their season is short. If you're lucky enough to have an opportunity to forage wild leeks, take full advantage of it, and try them in this dish. These go well with grilled meats like striploins (page 230).

SERVES 4

INGREDIENTS

8 leeks, white and light green parts only (or at least 16 wild leeks)

1 shallot, minced

4 Tbsp butter, cubed

Salt + freshly cracked pepper

2 to 4 tablespoons of grated Parmesan (optional)

HOW TO

Preheat the oven to 425°F. Line a baking sheet with parchment paper.

In a large, shallow fry pan, bring ½ cup of salted water to a boil. Blanch the leeks for 3 minutes or until slightly tender. Drain and immediately rinse under cold running water. Cut the leeks in half lengthwise (or, if using wild leeks, leave them whole). Pat dry.

Spread the leeks across the prepared baking sheet. Scatter the shallots overtop, top with the butter, and season with salt and pepper. Roast for 20 minutes or until the butter is brown and the leeks are softened. Add the Parmesan halfway through roasting for an extra kick of flavour.

COOK'S NOTE

There's usually a lot of dirt between the leeks' layers, so be sure to fan them out under cold running water to rinse away dirt and clean them well.

ROASTED ASPARAGUS WITH FETA + LEMON

As soon as the asparagus pokes up at my parents' farm, there's a lineup for it. I drive over, and cut my own. We'd eat it every night of its short season if we didn't have to share it with my siblings and the local restaurants. If you have the chance, visit a local roadside stand and load up. Use extras in risotto (page 186) or an omelette (page 168).

SERVES 6

INGREDIENTS

2 bunches asparagus, ends snapped off

3 Tbsp olive oil

Salt and freshly cracked pepper

¼ cup cubed or crumbled feta

2 Tbsp grated lemon zest (about 1 lemon)

HOW TO

Preheat the oven to 450°F. Peel the bottom third of the asparagus if it's thicker than the tip. Place the asparagus in a single layer on a baking sheet. Drizzle with 2 tablespoons of the olive oil, and season with salt and pepper.

Roast for 6 to 8 minutes, or until just tender. Add the feta and lemon and roast another 3 minutes or until the cheese bubbles and softens. Season with pepper, drizzle with the remaining olive oil, and serve.

ROASTED ASPARAGUS WITH PROSCIUTTO

This is a casual variation of wrapped asparagus, a *dish entertains* favourite hors d'oeuvre. It's faster, less fussy, and more family-focused than my original version. Serve this with the salmon (page 203) or pork chops (page 223), but it's almost a light meal on its own.

SERVES 4 TO 6

INGREDIENTS

20 spears asparagus, ends snapped off

1 Tbsp olive oil

½ cup grated Parmesan

5 slices prosciutto

Freshly cracked pepper

HOW TO

Preheat the oven to 450°F. Use a Y-peeler to trim the woody ends of the asparagus to create a uniform thickness. Place the asparagus in a single layer in a shallow gratin dish. Drizzle with the olive oil. Roast for about 5 minutes, or until just softened—the fresher and thinner the asparagus, the less time it will need.

Increase the oven temperature to 500°F. Sprinkle the asparagus with ¼ cup Parmesan. Cut each prosciutto slice into 4. Lay the prosciutto across the stem ends of the asparagus and sprinkle the remaining Parmesan over the prosciutto and the asparagus tips. Roast for another 3 to 4 minutes, until the cheese is bubbling.

ROASTED SESAME CARROTS

I was first introduced to za'atar and sumac by a guest chef during a cooking a class when I owned *dish*, and she made a Middle Eastern fattoush. I remember it as a more flavourful tomato bread salad. Recently, I was in a cool Syrian restaurant in Montreal, and their fattoush was very different. It was light, mostly green with hints of toasted pita, and powered by the smoky and earthy flavours of za'atar and sumac. I've added these spices to my list of pantry essentials. Both are amazing with carrots.

SERVES 2 TO 4

INGREDIENTS

1 tsp za'atar

1 Tbsp maple syrup

2 Tbsp olive oil

1 Tbsp sesame seeds

Salt + freshly cracked pepper

1 bunch thin carrots, tops trimmed + kept on, halved lengthwise

1 handful baby watercress, stems trimmed, or daikon or any microgreen

Plain Greek yogurt, for serving

HOW TO

Preheat the oven to 425°F.

In a bowl, combine the za'atar with the maple syrup, olive oil, sesame seeds, and some salt and pepper. Add the carrots and toss to coat. Spread the carrots out on a parchment-lined baking sheet or gratin dish. Roast for 30 to 40 minutes, or until soft and caramelized.

Top the carrots with the watercress and serve with yogurt on the side.

COOK'S NOTE

The maple syrup and sesame seeds will candy while in the oven.
If you're lucky, there will be a little extra pool you can devour as a sesame brittle.

HONEY ROASTED CARROTS

These are sticky-sweet with a touch of heat, and they're a welcome change after raw carrot consumption. Even the kids love them.

SERVES 4

INGREDIENTS

3 Tbsp honey

2 Tbsp olive oil

1 tsp smoked paprika

½ tsp chili flakes

1 lb/455 g carrots, tops trimmed + kept on

Salt + freshly cracked pepper

HOW TO

Preheat the oven to 425°F. Line 2 large baking sheets with parchment paper.

In a small bowl, combine the honey, olive oil, paprika, and chili flakes.

Spread the carrots out on the prepared baking sheets, and brush with enough of the oil and honey mixture to coat. Set aside the rest of the mixture for basting. Season the carrots with salt and pepper.

Roast the carrots for 20 minutes, and then use tongs to flip them. Roast for 10 more minutes, then baste with some of the remaining oil and honey mixture, and then continue to bake until the edges begin to caramelize and the carrots are cooked through, another 5 to 10 minutes.

CHILI GARLIC CHARD

This quick and healthy side is flavourful, pretty, and the perfect accompaniment to BBQ Maple Trout (page 202). Leftovers can be used in a risotto (page 186) or pasta.

SERVES 2 TO 4

INGREDIENTS

1 head rainbow chard, tough stems removed

2 Tbsp olive oil

2 cloves garlic

1 tsp chili flakes

Juice of ½ lemon

Salt + freshly cracked pepper

HOW TO

Trim off any remaining thicker stems from the chard. Set aside. Tear the chard into large pieces.

In a large pan over medium-high heat, heat the olive oil. Add the garlic and chili flakes and fry for 1 to 2 minutes until fragrant.

Add the stems, and sauté until they soften, about 3 minutes. Add the leaves, and sauté for 1 to 2 minutes until wilted. Drizzle with the lemon juice and season with salt and pepper before serving.

BROCCOLINI WITH FRIED CHILIES + SHALLOTS

We grew up eating steamed broccoli with butter. I later learned that broccoli has a large, extended family, and I have come to love every member of it. Broccoli's younger sibling is broccolini. It has longer stems and curled leaves, is long and thin, and doesn't have florets. Broccoli rabe, or rapini, is more bitter and is actually part of the turnip family. Spigarello is an heirloom variety of broccoli but also a parent of rabe. Chefs love spigarello for its earthiness, bitterness, and beauty. It's touted as a new alternative to kale. Try them all. This recipe is great with the trout on page 202.

SERVES 4

INGREDIENTS

1 bunch broccolini, spigarello, or broccoli rabe, chopped into long florets

1 Tbsp olive oil

1 tsp chili flakes

2 small shallots, minced

Zest + juice of 1 lemon

Salt + freshly cracked pepper

HOW TO

In a medium pot filled with salted boiling water, blanch the broccolini for 2 minutes. Drain and immediately plunge into a bowl of ice-cold water. Pat dry.

In a medium pan over medium-high heat, heat the olive oil. Add the chili flakes and sauté for a few minutes. Add the shallots and sauté until crispy, about 2 minutes. Add the broccolini and sauté about 5 minutes, or until softened.

Remove from the heat. Sprinkle with the lemon zest and juice and season with salt and pepper.

SECRET BBQ-CHARRED BROCCOLI

My friend Alex shared one of her favourite cookbooks with me, *Malibu Farm Cookbook*. Their restaurant at the pier is still on my bucket list to visit. I love the author's Latin-meets-surf laissez-faire cooking style, and she cooks with a lot of mayonnaise . . . and now I get why. Who knew grilling with mayonnaise as a marinade would be one of the most delicious things? I made this for a dinner party we hosted in Creemore. My friend Tori doesn't eat mayonnaise and she unknowingly gobbled this up. Add fried or roasted chickpeas (page 106) to this, and some Roasted Cauliflower + Ricotta Puree (page 54), and you've got yourself a meal.

SERVES 4

INGREDIENTS

1 head broccoli, cut into florets

½ cup mayonnaise, or enough to coat

Juice of 1 lemon

1 Tbsp sesame seeds (optional)

Freshly cracked pepper

HOW TO

Preheat the barbecue to high heat.

In a bowl, toss the broccoli florets with the mayonnaise, lemon juice, and sesame seeds (if using) until coated.

Place directly on the grill. Grill for about 10 to 15 minutes, turning the florets as they begin to char. Keep grilling until the florets are softened and just charred.

Remove from the grill and season with pepper. Enjoy.

COOK'S NOTE

If you're still turning your nose up at the idea of grilling with mayonnaise, try using ½ cup ricotta.

OVEN-ROASTED CHERRY TOMATOES

Each summer I find our vegetable garden is a learning experience. I don't have a green thumb . . . so I call my dad for help. But it's also fun to learn from trial and error. One year we went a bit over the top with the tomatoes. I planted endless varieties. I also crammed them all in a bit too close so they didn't get the space and light they needed and were less than perfect. My dad's specialty orange sun sugar variety (sweet and hard to find), were a home run.

SERVES 4

INGREDIENTS

1 pint yellow and orange cherry tomatoes

1 Tbsp olive oil

4 sprigs thyme, leaves only

Salt + freshly cracked pepper

1 (5 oz/140 g) package goat cheese, softened

HOW TO

Preheat the oven to 450°F. Place the tomatoes on a parchment-lined baking sheet or small ovenproof gratin dish. Drizzle with the olive oil, layer with the sprigs of thyme, and generously season with salt and pepper. Roast for about 15 minutes or until the tomatoes pop and shrivel.

To assemble, spread the goat cheese in a small 8-inch round, shallow gratin dish, then spoon the warm tomatoes overtop. Serve with a plate of toasts on the side.

COOK'S NOTE

Serve this very casually, bar-snack–style; give everyone a little plate and embrace a messy self-serve approach. If you are in a rush and don't have time to bring the goat cheese to room temperature, bake it at 450°F for a few minutes until warmed through. You can swap out the goat cheese with the same amount of room-temperature crumbled feta. Try sprinkling with some roughly chopped pistachios on top for a little crunch.

YAMATO-STYLE VEGGIE FRIED RICE

For birthdays, it's become a family ritual for us to celebrate and gather around the grill at Yamato, a family-favourite Japanese restaurant in Toronto. Their dramatic, theatrical cooking demonstration makes the guest of honour, and the whole family, feel special. It's from these pros that we all learned how to perfect veggie fried rice. It's a crowd-pleaser, even though my kids always say, "That's not exactly how Yamato does it." Enjoy with chicken, fish, or steak.

SERVES 6

INGREDIENTS

2 cups jasmine or basmati rice

2 Tbsp vegetable oil

1 small onion, cut into small dice

1 red bell pepper, cut into small dice

1 zucchini, cut into small dice

1 head broccoli, cut into small florets + blanched

4 eggs

Salt + freshly cracked pepper

4 green onions, white + light green parts only, thinly sliced on an angle

Sesame seeds, dry-toasted

1 Tbsp soy sauce

2 Tbsp butter, room temperature

2 tsp wasabi, or to taste (optional)

HOW TO

Cook the rice according to the package instructions. Drain and set aside.

In a large skillet over medium-high heat, heat the vegetable oil. Add the onions and sauté for 2 minutes until they are soft and translucent. Add the bell peppers, zucchini, and broccoli, and fry a few more minutes until softened. Turn down the heat to medium. Add the rice and fry a few minutes, folding in the vegetables until combined.

In a small bowl, whisk the eggs and season with salt and pepper. Create a well in the rice, pour the eggs into the well, and stir to incorporate. Remove from the heat; the residual heat of the pan will cook the egg. Mix in the green onions and sesame seeds, and finish with soy sauce.

In a small bowl, mix together the butter and wasabi (if using). Fold the wasabi mixture into the rice before serving.

POTATO + GREEN TOMATO GRATIN

I had visions of being part of the kitchen in *Fried Green Tomatoes* despite my nonexistent Southern roots. I now have an American cousin—a good cook to boot—who I hope will approve of my nod to the movie's classic dish. It's hard to find green tomatoes in Toronto. I was never really clear on whether green tomatoes were their own variety or just unripe red tomatoes. The short version is that they're both. Green tomatoes often have stripes, look heirloom, and are soft to the touch when they ripen (save true heirloom tomatoes for a fresh platter). Try this alongside Southern-Baked Chicken (page 216).

SERVES 4

INGREDIENTS

½ cup chicken stock

¼ cup whipping cream

¼ cup grated Parmesan

1 clove garlic, minced

1 Tbsp chopped rosemary

Salt + freshly cracked pepper

2 Tbsp butter, cold, cubed

3 large russet potatoes, peeled + thinly sliced with a mandoline

5 large green tomatoes, thinly sliced

HOW TO

Preheat the oven to 400°F.

In a bowl, mix together the stock, cream, Parmesan, garlic, and rosemary, and season with salt and pepper.

For the first layer, place half of the butter cubes on the bottom of a large 12-inch round gratin dish and add a single layer of the potatoes. Season with salt and pepper. Pour the stock mixture overtop, then add a layer of tomatoes.

Use the remaining potatoes on the next layer, followed by the remaining tomatoes. Pour the remaining stock mixture overtop.

Bake for 25 minutes or until the potatoes are soft and the top is golden. If the cheese starts to brown too soon—about halfway through baking time—you may need to cover the dish with aluminum foil. Remove from the oven and let sit for a few minutes before serving.

COOK'S NOTE

You can use unripe red tomatoes instead of green, like I did for this photo (pop them in a paper bag on a sunny windowsill to soften a bit). For a more rustic version, keep the potato skins on.

OVEN-ROASTED CORN

This recipe is a great way to have corn every night, even in the off-season. Use frozen corn kernels for a side that brings you back to summer. Load it with avocados, roasted tomatoes, and more veggies to turn it into a salad. This is delicious with Southern-Baked Chicken (page 216) or BBQ Sticky Ribs (page 225).

SERVES 4

INGREDIENTS

4 cobs corn, or 4 cups frozen corn kernels, thawed

1 poblano pepper, deseeded, stem removed + minced

4 tsp butter, cut into small cubes

Salt + freshly cracked pepper

HOW TO

Preheat the oven to 450°F. Line a baking sheet with parchment paper. If using fresh corn, remove the kernels from the cobs.

Spread the corn kernels out on the prepared pan. Scatter with the poblano, top with the butter, and season with salt and pepper. Roast for 10 to 15 minutes or until the kernels are softened and browned. Serve warm.

COOK'S NOTE

Poblanos are milder than jalapenos (see page 42), but you can use a jalapeno for a hotter result, or try ½ teaspoon of chili flakes if you have them in your pantry. You could also add half a sliced red onion and half a pint of halved grape tomatoes to roast with the corn for a more diverse warm side, or dress the corn with juice of 1 lime and 1 tablespoon olive oil for a cold salad in summer.

CREAMY MUSHROOMS

While this is a perfect side, it's also great as a topping for your favourite grilled meat or chicken. The mushrooms shrivel, so you may want to double the recipe if this is your only side.

SERVES 2 TO 4

INGREDIENTS

2 Tbsp butter

¼ cup finely diced shallots

4 cups assorted mushrooms (such as cremini, porcini, button), finely diced

3 sprigs thyme, leaves removed + chopped

¼ cup white wine

⅓ cup whipping cream

Salt + freshly cracked pepper

HOW TO

In a large skillet over medium heat, melt the butter. Add the shallots, and sauté for a few minutes until softened. Add the mushrooms and thyme, and sauté until the mushrooms dry out and the liquid evaporates, about 5 minutes.

Increase the heat to high. Deglaze the pan with the wine, stirring up any bits that have stuck to the bottom of the pan and incorporating them. Stir in the cream. Simmer for a few minutes, stirring occasionally, until the mixture thickens. Season with salt and pepper.

COOK'S NOTE

George Butterfield, founder of the travel company, Butterfield and Robinson, always says "life's too short to drink bad wine." I feel the same about cooking with wine; cook with what you like to drink.

BRUSSELS SPROUTS
WITH PANCETTA + DATES

I remember the first time I had Brussels sprouts. I was in grade nine and at a friend's house. Her mom made me eat them, and I hated them. Oh, how I've changed. The Niagara Street Grill, way back when, taught me to love all veggies thanks to their amazing sides. This recipe is a great side mostly because of the maple syrup and balsamic vinegar that candy the sprouts. And now it's one that I feed to the friends of my kids. I tell them, "If I make you eat your veggies, it means I love you and you are like family."

SERVES 4

INGREDIENTS

5 oz/140 g pancetta, cut into chunks

1 lb/455 g Brussels sprouts

2 Tbsp olive oil

Salt + freshly cracked pepper

3 Tbsp aged balsamic vinegar

2 Tbsp maple syrup

½ cup Medjool dates, pitted + halved

HOW TO

Preheat the oven to 425°F.

In a pan over medium heat, fry the pancetta for 2 to 3 minutes per side until it crisps and curls.

In a shallow baking dish or sheet pan lined with parchment paper, toss the Brussels sprouts with the olive oil. Season with salt and pepper. Roast for 10 minutes. Drizzle with the balsamic and maple syrup and toss to coat. Top with the dates and pancetta, and roast for 10 more minutes or until just softened. Place under the broiler for about 30 seconds at the end to caramelize.

Season with salt and pepper and serve.

COOK'S NOTE

For added richness, top while hot with a few dollops of Gorgonzola or your favourite blue cheese, just before serving.

ROASTED EGGPLANT WITH JAMMY TOMATOES

Eggplant needs salt to draw the bitterness out. But once it's roasted and the flavour is balanced out with sweetness and other tastes, it melts in your mouth. When I was younger, my friend Dave's mom used to make tender and jammy ratatouille. She'd make it look effortless, throwing tomatoes, eggplant, and garlic in a slow cooker before walking out the door. Ottolenghi's roasted eggplant with buttermilk and pomegranate became my new favourite way to eat eggplant. This recipe combines the best of both: it's a classic ratatouille taste with a pretty presentation.

SERVES 4

INGREDIENTS

2 long eggplants

¼ cup + 1 Tbsp olive oil

2 Tbsp maple syrup

4 sprigs thyme, leaves only

Salt + freshly cracked pepper

2 Roma tomatoes, cut into large dice

1 Tbsp olive oil

1 Tbsp aged balsamic vinegar

¼ cup creamy goat cheese

½ cup plain yogurt

Zest + juice of 1 lemon

½ cup pine nuts, toasted

HOW TO

Preheat the oven to 400°F. Line a baking sheet with parchment paper.

Cut the eggplants lengthwise. Starting at the top and from one side to the other, cut 6 "V" shapes into the flesh, without cutting through the skin. Place the eggplants cut-side up on the prepared sheet. Brush them with the ¼ cup of olive oil and then with the maple syrup. Sprinkle with the thyme, and season with salt and pepper. Roast for 30 to 40 minutes, or until softened and browned.

In a small gratin dish, toss the tomatoes with the remaining 1 tablespoon olive oil and the balsamic. While the eggplants are cooking, roast the tomatoes for 15 to 20 minutes, or until the tomatoes are jammy.

In a bowl, mix together the goat cheese, yogurt, and lemon zest and juice. Set aside.

To serve, top the eggplants with the tomatoes and yogurt mixture. Sprinkle with the toasted pine nuts.

CHILI-LIME ROASTED SWEET POTATO FRIES

This recipe is how I got the family to finally accept sweet potato fries in place of regular fries. Enough said.

SERVES 4

INGREDIENTS

Sweet Potato Fries:

2 large sweet potatoes, peeled, sliced in half lengthwise + cut into matchsticks

2 Tbsp olive oil

2 Tbsp maple syrup

Zest + juice of ½ lime

1 tsp chili powder

Salt + freshly cracked pepper

Chipotle Aioli:

2 Tbsp mayonnaise

1 tsp minced chipotle in adobo

Juice of ½ lime (about 1 Tbsp)

Topping:

2 green onions, white + light green parts only, thinly sliced on the diagonal

Flaked sea salt

HOW TO

Preheat the oven to 400°F. Line a sheet pan with parchment paper.

In a bowl, toss the sweet potatoes with the olive oil, maple syrup, lime zest and juice, chili powder, and salt and pepper to coat. Spread the potatoes out on the prepared pan. Roast for 30 minutes or until the potatoes are brown and tips are crispy.

Meanwhile, make the chipotle aioli. In a small bowl, combine the mayonnaise with the minced chipotle. Stir in the lime juice.

Top the fries with the green onions and a sprinkle of flaked salt. Serve with the chipotle aioli on the side.

COOK'S NOTE

Store the leftover chipotle in adobo in a small airtight jar in the fridge and use in chicken lettuce wraps (page 218) the next day.

ODE TO STUFFED BAKERS SMASHED POTATOES

This is another of our new family favourites. It's definitely worth adding to your weekly menu rotation. The kids like making these and they do a perfect job. Try these alongside the pork chops (page 223).

SERVES 6

INGREDIENTS

2 lb/900 g baby Yukon gold potatoes, unpeeled

1 cup Greek yogurt

2 Tbsp minced dill

2 Tbsp sliced chives

2 green onions, white + light green parts only, sliced

Juice of ½ lemon

1 tsp honey

Salt + freshly cracked pepper

2 Tbsp olive oil

HOW TO

Preheat the oven to 450°F. Line a baking sheet with parchment paper.

In a large pot over medium-high heat, cover the potatoes with water and add a generous amount of salt. Bring to a boil, and boil until the potatoes are just soft, about 10 to 15 minutes.

In a small bowl, combine the yogurt, dill, chives (reserving some of both herbs for garnish), green onions, lemon juice, and honey. Season with salt and pepper and set aside.

Drain the potatoes and let cool enough to handle. Place the potatoes on the prepared sheet. Using the palm of your hand, flatten the potatoes. Drizzle with the olive oil and season with salt and pepper. Roast for 30 minutes or until crisp on the bottom.

To serve, top the potatoes with the yogurt mixture and the reserved dill and chives.

COOK'S NOTE

For a meatier version, fry chunks of pancetta in a cast-iron pan until crispy.

MAINS
Eggs, Pasta + Risotto, Pizza + Tacos

Eggs

Pasta + Risotto

Pizza

Tacos

LESSONS FROM A NOVICE GARDENER

When you start your own garden or want to expand your gardening expertise, it's great to have teachers to learn from. Mine are my mom and dad. My dad is a large-scale gardening expert with boundless energy who has learned from years of successes and failures. My mom likes to garden herbs and flowers on a smaller scale. They both learned from trial and error with wisdom shared from farmer Kate, a local organic farmer with a deep love for and understanding of the land. My dad passed on his learnings to our neighbour Anne, who shared them with our other neighbour Sara, who shared with Laurie, who inspired Mindy ... And so it goes. We all love to learn from each other, and we all use *The Vegetable Gardener's Bible* for reference.

When planning your garden, consider your space. Patios and smaller spaces can be ideal places to pot and grow peppers, herbs, tomatoes, and lettuces—try growing these in a small tub on your sill or outdoor perch. Roomy backyards or country living allow for a raised bed or two to experiment with potatoes, beets, chard, and carrots. Large field areas are great for asparagus, zucchini, and other

members of the squash family, including watermelon, as they are wild at heart and need space to spread. Some vegetables are higher-maintenance, like tomatoes, which need to be pinched off so they don't grow out of control. Some vegetables need support: peas need chicken wire to grab hold of, and peppers and beans need stake support as they grow.

There's a science for what to plant and when: after the last frost in spring, plant carrots, radishes, beets, and lettuces from seed; when the late spring heat arrives, plant tomatoes, peppers, and cucumber seedlings. Follow the seed packaging guidelines and adjust based on where you live. Like people, some vegetables belong together. Others don't. Like potatoes and onions.

Remember to seek guidance from your local experts and community of family, friends, and neighbours. A garden is a little like life: sometimes you fail, sometimes you succeed, but you rarely regret trying new things.

SPRING GOAT CHEESE + ASPARAGUS OMELETTE

Fin has mastered the omelette—it's an important dish to teach the teenagers before they leave the nest; their wallets will thank you. This particular recipe is perfect for a weekend brunch or lunch or a midweek dinner. The eggs cook quickly and won't wait for you to slice and dice your omelette fixings, so have your mise en place prepped and ready to go. Cook the eggs on medium-low heat so you don't colour them. Once you get comfortable working with this heat, you'll become an omelette master, like Fin.

SERVES 2

INGREDIENTS

4 eggs

2 Tbsp cold water or milk

Salt + freshly cracked pepper

1 Tbsp butter

4 spears asparagus, chopped (separate the stems from tips) + blanched

2 green onions, white + light green part only, thinly sliced

2 to 3 Tbsp crumbled goat cheese

Salsa, hot sauce, or tomato butter, for serving

HOW TO

In a small bowl, whisk together the eggs, cold water, and salt and pepper.

In a medium nonstick pan over medium-low heat, melt the butter. Add the asparagus stems and green onions, and sauté for 2 minutes. Pour in the egg mixture, allowing it to spread out and cover the bottom of the pan. Cook for 2 minutes or until just set. You don't want to overcook or allow the eggs to get any colour.

Place the asparagus tips on one side of the eggs, sprinkle with the cheese, and season with salt and pepper. Using a wooden spatula, fold the egg into thirds. As you flip the final third, roll it out onto the plate to close it up. Serve with your favourite salsa on the side.

COOK'S NOTE

*Cold water in omelettes makes for a slightly thinner texture and milk
makes them a bit creamier. Try adding a handful of baby spinach along
with the green onions. In the summer, swap out the asparagus for a diced tomato.
In the fall, substitute the asparagus with ½ cup chopped mushrooms, and
the goat cheese with 2 to 3 tablespoons Parmesan. Equal amounts of
Boursin is a great alternative to the goat cheese.*

BAKED EGGS WITH ROASTED TOMATOES + SPINACH

This recipe is as easy and fast as scrambled eggs, but more impressive and delicious. The secret is in the baking. I first tried baked eggs with olive oil and grilled bread at New York's Standard Grill in the Meatpacking District many years ago and kept coming back for them. When I finally tried making baked eggs at home, I realized how simple it was.

SERVES 2 TO 4

INGREDIENTS

2 Tbsp olive oil

2 small Roma tomatoes, sliced lengthwise, or ½ cup halved cherry tomatoes

1 cup roughly torn spinach, stems trimmed

4 eggs

Salt + freshly cracked pepper

4 slices sourdough bread

Flaked sea salt

2 Tbsp aged balsamic vinegar

1 cup frisée (optional)

HOW TO

Preheat the oven to 425°F. Use half the olive oil to grease a small gratin dish or 4 ramekins. Place the tomatoes in the dish or divide among the ramekins, then layer with spinach. Crack the eggs into the dish or ramekins. Season with salt and pepper. Bake for 10 minutes, or until the egg whites are set and the yolks are still runny. The eggs will continue to cook in the hot dish once it's out of the oven.

While the eggs are cooking, place the bread on a baking sheet and bake for about 5 minutes, until toasted. Season the toast with salt and drizzle with half the balsamic vinegar.

In a bowl, toss the frisée (if using) with the remaining oil and vinegar. To serve, place the frisée on the grilled breads, and slide the eggs on top.

COOK'S NOTE

Try adding 1 sliced green onion to the base with the spinach; or adding a slice of ham or prosciutto before the frisée; or serving with a dollop of salsa and sliced avocado. Substitute chopped Swiss chard for the spinach, or top the eggs with crumbled feta before putting them in the oven. The options are endless.

THE SKINNY ON PASTA

Dried and fresh pasta are both essential items. Dried pasta is ideal for dishes where you want to load up on sauce and fixings. Fresh pasta is better for simpler dishes, like an arrabiata. You can't beat dried pasta for convenience, but fresh pasta freezes beautifully, and you can cook it right from frozen.

SPAGHETTI LIMONE

This is an ode to Terroni's Spaghetti al Limone. After years of ordering it, I thought I would add it to my own cooking roster at home and try more complex dishes when I'm in the restaurant. Quality Parmesan is key to success for this simple dish.

SERVES 4

INGREDIENTS

¼ cup olive oil

Zest + juice of 2 lemons

1 lb/455 g dried spaghetti

⅓ cup grated Parmesan + extra to garnish

⅓ cup shaved Parmesan + extra to garnish

⅓ cup capers

Freshly cracked pepper

Pinch of hot chilies, or to taste (optional)

HOW TO

Bring a large pot of salted water to a boil. In a bowl, whisk together the oil and lemon zest and juice.

Add the pasta to the boiling water and cook according to the package instructions until al dente. Just before you drain it, take a 2-cup measure and reserve about 1 cup of the pasta water.

Drain the pasta, return it to the pot, and toss with the lemon mixture. If necessary, add some of the pasta water, a little at a time, until you reach your desired consistency. Stir in both Parmesans and the capers. Season with pepper.

To serve, season with more pepper, and top with more cheese and the chilies (if using).

COOK'S NOTE

*Using a combination of shaved and grated Parmesan means
the grated cheese doesn't get lost in the sauce.*

QUICK-BLISTERED TOMATO TAGLIATELLE

This simple dish shows how minimal ingredients can let the beauty of fresh pasta shine. I order fresh pasta weekly in my Mama Earth Organics boxes and often double the amount I think I'll need, as it freezes so nicely.

SERVES 4

INGREDIENTS

3 Tbsp olive oil

2 cloves garlic

1 pint cherry tomatoes

1 package fresh tagliatelle

1 handful arugula or pea shoot microgreens

¼ cup chopped basil

¼ cup grated Parmesan

Salt + freshly cracked pepper

HOW TO

In a heavy cast-iron pan over medium-high heat, heat 2 tablespoons olive oil and fry the garlic for 1 minute. Add the tomatoes and sauté until they burst, soften, and blister, about 10 minutes. Set aside.

Bring a large pot of salted water to a boil. Cook the pasta according to the package instructions. Just before draining, take a 2-cup measure and reserve about 1 cup of the pasta water. Drain the pasta.

In a large bowl, toss the warm pasta with the tomatoes. If necessary, add pasta water, a little at a time, until you reach your desired consistency. Top with the greens, basil, and Parmesan and season generously with salt and pepper. Drizzle with the remaining olive oil.

BACON + PEA FUSILLI

This is a cottage family favourite perfected by my mom and sister-in-law, Amanda. The whole family loves it. Olivia asks for this comfort pasta when she's wanting some simple home cooking. We all love a creamy dish and are unapologetic about our love of cream. My grandmother insists flavour comes from fat. My mom says, "Enjoy it and work it off." They are both right, as always.

SERVES 4

INGREDIENTS

8 to 10 slices bacon

2 shallots, finely diced

½ cup white wine

2 cups whipping cream

1 cup fresh baby peas

6 sage leaves

½ cup chicken stock

1 handful spinach, washed, dried + stems removed (optional)

4 cups fusilli

½ cup grated Parmesan

Salt + freshly cracked pepper

HOW TO

In a large sauté pan over medium-low heat, fry the bacon until crisp. Set aside. Cut the bacon into bite-size pieces. Remove the bacon fat from the pan, reserving 1 tablespoon in the pan. In the same pan over medium heat, sauté the shallots for a few minutes until softened. Increase the heat to high and deglaze with the wine, scraping up any bits that have stuck to the bottom of the pan and incorporating them.

Stir in the cream and then the stock, and turn the heat back down to medium. Cook the sauce for 3 to 5 minutes until it starts to thicken. Add the bacon, peas, and sage and cook for 3 more minutes, until the sauce is thickened. Add the spinach and turn off the heat.

Meanwhile, bring a large pot of salted water to a boil, and cook the pasta according to the package instructions. Just before draining, take a 2-cup measure and reserve about 1 cup of the pasta water. Drain the pasta. Add the pasta to the sauce, and stir to combine. The sauce should be thick and creamy. If necessary, add some of the pasta water, a little at a time, until the desired consistency is reached. Sprinkle with the Parmesan and season with pepper.

COOK'S NOTE

*In the spring, add a bunch of asparagus, trimmed and chopped, stems and tips,
or about a cup of sugar snap peas. The spinach wilts up, so the kids won't even notice.*

GREEN MAC + CHEESE

Charlotte might be too old for Dr. Seuss's *Green Eggs and Ham*, but the question "What's that green in the pasta?" seems to be ageless. Luckily, this foolproof mac and cheese may be green but it still has the approval of my kids. This recipe is great for a hungry crowd, and gives you welcome leftovers to simply reheat for lunch the next day.

SERVES 6

INGREDIENTS

Pasta + Sauce:
3 Tbsp butter
3 Tbsp all-purpose flour
Salt + freshly cracked pepper
2½ cups milk
½ tsp dry mustard powder
½ tsp cayenne pepper

1½ cups grated extra-old cheddar
¼ cup mayonnaise
3 cups fusilli or penne
2 cups baby spinach
1 cup broccoli florets

Topping:
1 cup ½ inch-cubed day-old bread
⅓ cup grated Parmesan
½ tsp paprika
2 Tbsp butter, melted
Tomato chili sauce or hot sauce, for serving

HOW TO

Preheat the oven to 375°F.

For the sauce, in a medium saucepan over medium heat, melt the butter. Stir in the flour, season with salt and pepper, and cook for 2 minutes, stirring constantly. Gradually add the milk, stirring constantly. Add the mustard and cayenne. Cook, stirring often, until thickened, about 5 minutes. Remove from the heat and stir in the cheddar and mayonnaise. Set aside.

Bring a large pot of salted water to a boil, and cook the pasta according to the package instructions. In the final minute of boiling, add the broccoli to blanch it. Drain the pasta and broccoli and return them to the pot. Stir in the cheese sauce. Pour the mixture into a 9- × 13-inch casserole dish. Stir in the spinach.

To make the topping, in a small bowl, combine the cubed bread, Parmesan, and paprika. Stir in the melted butter. Evenly spread the topping over the pasta.

Bake for 20 minutes or until the top is bubbling. Place under the broiler for 3 minutes or until the top is golden brown. Serve with your favourite tomato chili sauce.

COTTAGE LASAGNA

This lasagna was my sister-in-law, Amanda's, mom's specialty. Mrs. Wendy liked to gather with family and friends and take care of people with good food, drinks, and fun, just like my mom . . . traits both Amanda and I have inherited. But Amanda wins as domestic goddess in our extended family. She usually shows up at the cottage with a few family-size lasagnas that would have taken her all afternoon to prepare. We love and appreciate her for it. This recipe has been adapted over the years, adding a new béchamel layer. Her instructions were loose and the results would have fed an army. This is now finely tuned to make two lasagnas, so you can freeze one in a deep glass, freezer-proof dish with a lid. This recipe is the best lasagna I have ever had, but it does take a bit of work: a worthwhile labour of love.

MAKES TWO 9- × 12-INCH LASAGNAS, SERVES 12

INGREDIENTS

Meat Sauce:

2 lb/900 g lean ground beef

Salt + freshly cracked pepper

1 cup finely chopped mushrooms

2 (22 oz/660 ml each) jars tomato sauce (I like Raos)

Cottage Cheese + Spinach Layer:

1 (18 oz/500 g) container cottage cheese

1 egg, lightly beaten

2 cups fresh baby spinach, roughly chopped (or 2 cups frozen spinach, thawed and drained)

Salt + freshly cracked pepper

Béchamel Cheese Sauce:

¼ cup butter

¼ cup all-purpose flour

2 cups milk

Salt + freshly cracked pepper

2 cups grated aged cheddar

Assembly:

2 (1 lb/455 g each) packages oven-ready lasagna noodles

2 (14 oz/400 g) bricks mozzarella

1 cup finely grated Parmesan

COOK'S NOTE

Get a bunch of boxes of oven-ready lasagna noodles for the pantry in case you make extra lasagna to freeze. If you don't use them they'll be there for the next time. Oven-ready means you don't have to cook them first before assembly, so it's far less fussy, faster, and less messy—be sure to read the box to get the right type.

You could double up on the cottage cheese layer and eliminate the béchamel layer if you are in a pinch, but a fully loaded version is best.

For the meat sauce, in an extra-large sauté pan over medium heat, cook the ground beef until browned. Season generously with salt and pepper. Add the mushrooms and sauté for a few minutes. Stir in the tomato sauce. Turn down the heat to low and simmer for 10 minutes until the mixture has reduced, cooked, and thickened. Set aside.

For the cottage cheese and spinach layer, in a medium bowl, mix the cottage cheese with the egg. Stir in the chopped spinach, season with salt and pepper, and set aside.

For the béchamel cheese sauce, in a medium saucepan over medium heat, melt the butter and then add the flour. Stirring constantly, let the flour cook for a few minutes; be sure not to burn it. Whisk in the milk, and keep whisking until the mixture thickens and starts to bubble, about 5 minutes. If it's thickening too fast, you can add a bit more milk, 1 tablespoon at a time. Season with salt and pepper. Remove from the heat and stir in the grated cheddar until it has melted. Start assembling the lasagna now so the sauce doesn't harden.

To assemble the lasagnas, set out two 9- × 12-inch casserole dishes. Layer each casserole dish the same, like an assembly line. First, pour a very small amount of the meat sauce into each dish to just cover the bottom. This prevents the noodles from sticking to it.

Then add a layer of noodles. You may need to snap the ends to make them fit. You can use the broken bits to fill in any of the layers as needed. Evenly spread a layer of meat sauce to cover the noodles entirely. Sprinkle a third of the mozzarella overtop.

Add another layer of noodles, pressing to push them down. Then spread the cottage cheese and spinach over them, ensuring the entire noodle layer is covered. Add another layer of meat sauce, and sprinkle with more mozzarella.

Add another layer of noodles, pressing to push them down again. Pour half of the béchamel cheese sauce overtop of each dish and spread evenly over the noodles. Cover with a final layer of noodles. Add more meat sauce, spreading it evenly across the noodles. Generously top the lasagnas with the rest of the mozzarella and sprinkle with the Parmesan. Wrap and freeze if you're not baking them right away.

When ready to bake, preheat the oven to 350°F. Bake for 45 minutes to 1 hour, until the sauce is bubbling and the top is browned. If baking from frozen, either take them out in the morning to thaw and bake as directed, or bake directly from frozen for about 1½ hours.

SWISS CHARD RISOTTO

Risotto is a simple dish, but also easy to mess up. It's the first meal Fin learned how to cook (despite abandoning the dry burning rice). In North America, Arborio rice is typically used. In Italy, more choices abound, like Vialone Nano or Carnaroli. Use a wide-bottomed sauté pan to uniformly toast the rice in a single layer and absorb the liquid. It requires small, regular additions of good-quality stock or broth. It also needs salt, which comes from the stock as well as the Parmesan. Use the best Parmesan you can find to finish at the end. Risotto allows you to slow down in the kitchen and enjoy a glass of wine while stirring.

SERVES 3 TO 4

INGREDIENTS

6 cups chicken stock

3 Tbsp butter

2 Tbsp olive oil

1 medium sweet onion, finely diced

1½ cups Arborio, Vialone Nano, or Carnaroli rice

½ cup white wine

1 bunch Swiss chard, stems + leaves chopped

¾ cup grated Parmesan

Freshly cracked pepper

HOW TO

In a medium saucepan over medium-low heat, bring the stock to a gentle simmer and keep it warm over low heat.

In a large sauté pan over medium heat, melt 2 tablespoons of the butter and heat the olive oil. Add the onions and sauté, stirring often, until soft but not brown, about 5 minutes. Stir in the rice. Fry, stirring often, for a few minutes until translucent. Add the wine and, stirring constantly, let the liquid cook off, about 2 minutes.

Add about ½ cup of stock at a time, keeping it at a steady simmer so the rice doesn't cook too quickly on the outside. Stir constantly until almost all the stock has been absorbed but the rice is not dry, about 2 minutes, then stir in another ½ cup of stock. Carry on stirring in the stock, ½ cup at a time, until the rice is soft and creamy but with a slight bite to it and there's still some liquid in the pan. This will take about 20 minutes in total (and you may not use all the stock). At the 15-minute point, stir in the chard stems. Once they soften, add the chopped chard leaves and cook until they're softened but still vibrant. That will only take a few minutes.

Remove from the heat. Stir in the remaining 1 tablespoon of butter and ½ cup of the Parmesan. Season with pepper. Stir again, then serve immediately, topped with the remaining Parmesan, or more to your liking.

SEASONAL VARIATIONS

Spring: *Add 1 to 2 cups fresh peas or a bunch of asparagus trimmed and roughly chopped, along with the chard stems.*

Summer: *Add 1 pint cherry tomatoes halfway through cooking time, and then the chopped meat from a lobster tail when you add the chard leaves, cooking until the lobster is cooked through.*

Fall: *Add 1½ cups chopped mixed forest mushrooms after you've sautéed the onions, allowing them to cook a few minutes. Add 1 cup shredded raw beets with the chard.*

Winter: *Add 1 cup rehydrated chopped dried mushrooms after you've sautéed the onions. Add 1 to 2 cups blanched, chopped broccoli rabe with the chard stems.*

THE SKINNY ON PIZZA

I wish I was a pizza dough and pastry expert, but I'm not. When we visit Peter's sister Karen and brother-in-law Michel, they make homemade dough look effortless, and pizza that tastes incredible straight from the grill. I rely on shortcuts to get an easy crust every time: We buy fresh dough from the pasta shop, or use frozen pizza dough balls, naan, or flatbreads from the grocery store. With local toppings, it's all delicious in the end. Or we order in from the pros at our local favourites, Nove or Terroni, when it's cooks' night off. On the next pages, I give you 2 easy pizza recipes—BBQ Pizza Bianco (above), and Potato, Leek + Gorgonzola (right)—for making pizza in the oven or on the grill.

POTATO, LEEK + GORGONZOLA PIZZA

Naan and flatbread are the perfect freezer-friendly staples for a quick and delicious midweek dinner. Lay out the prepped ingredients so everyone can customize their own pizza before baking in the oven (or throwing on the grill).

MAKES 2 LARGE PIZZAS

INGREDIENTS

4 to 6 small white potatoes

2 rectangular flatbreads

2 cloves garlic, minced

2 Tbsp olive oil

7 oz/200 g Gorgonzola

1 to 2 leeks, white parts only, halved lengthwise + sliced very thinly, or ½ red onion, sliced very thinly

6 slices prosciutto (optional)

½ cup grated Parmesan

2 sprigs rosemary, leaves only, finely chopped

Freshly cracked pepper

HOW TO

Preheat the oven to 450°F or heat the barbecue to medium-high.

Bring a large pot of salted water to a boil. Add the potatoes and boil until just tender, about 10 minutes. Run them under cold water to cool and then slice them very thinly.

Place the flatbreads on a baking sheet. In a small bowl, combine the garlic and olive oil. Brush the garlic-oil mixture onto the flatbreads. Divide the potato slices evenly between the flatbreads. Break the Gorgonzola into large pieces and add it to the flatbreads, along with the leeks and prosciutto (if using). Sprinkle with the Parmesan, rosemary, and pepper.

Bake for about 8 to 10 minutes in the oven, or 5 to 7 minutes directly on the grill, depending on your barbecue, until the flatbreads are crisp and the tops are bubbly.

COOK'S NOTE

This makes a great vegetarian pizza if you skip the prosciutto. You can also ditch the flatbreads and layer the toppings in a gratin dish for a gluten-free side. Substitute the rosemary with 2 sprigs of thyme. Brush a few tablespoons of pesto over the flatbreads for another layer of flavour.

BBQ PIZZA BIANCO

This is a quick midweek pizza. It's delicious when grilled directly on the barbecue, or it can be baked in the oven. This is a summer pizza but don't be afraid to use frozen corn in the colder months.

MAKES 4 SMALL PIZZAS

INGREDIENTS

1 cup fresh or frozen corn, thawed

2 Tbsp + 1 tsp olive oil

Salt + freshly cracked black pepper

1 cup ricotta

1 cup grated mozzarella

½ cup grated Parmesan

2 Tbsp chopped rosemary

3 sprigs thyme, leaves only, finely chopped

4 naan

½ sweet or Vidalia onion, thinly sliced

HOW TO

Preheat the oven to 400°F. Spread out the corn kernels on a baking sheet. Toss with 1 teaspoon of the oil, and season with salt and pepper. Bake for 10 minutes or until the kernels are browned and softened. Increase the oven temperature to 450°F (if baking the pizza) or heat the barbecue to medium-high.

In a bowl, combine the ricotta, mozzarella, Parmesan, 1 tablespoon of the oil, the rosemary, and thyme. Season with salt and pepper.

Brush the naan with the remaining olive oil. Spread the cheese mixture evenly over each naan. Top with the onions and scatter with the roasted corn.

Grill or bake the pizza until the edges are puffy and brown with a slight char and the underside is brown and fairly crisp, about 5 to 7 minutes on the grill, depending on your barbecue (or 8 to 10 minutes in the oven).

TACOS

Close to Creemore is Collingwood, a town filled with creative entrepreneurs and evolving craft beverage and food concepts. Wineries and distilleries are hidden on back roads, and indie coffee shops and casual restaurants are thriving across town. Bent Taco is one of my favourites. I don't know if it's the warm and kind culture, the delicious tacos, the outdoor patio, or the fact that we sit in ski clothes, drink beer, and linger midday, but it makes me feel younger and cooler just by being there. These tacos are a very loose interpretation of those served at Bent Taco, perfect for the midweek cook.

The beauty of tacos is that you can make them to your liking and do some of the assembly ahead of time. Select your favourite filling (here are four to choose from), and pair it with your favourite fixings, listed below. You will only need part of the Taco Slaw, Pickled Onions, and Pickled Cucumbers recipes for your tacos).

MAKES 8 TACOS

INGREDIENTS

Fillings:
Fillings of your choice
  (pages 194 to 199)

Fixing Options:
Taco Slaw (page 87)
Pickled Onions (page 40)

Pickled Cucumbers
  (page 40)
½ red or yellow bell
  pepper, thinly sliced
Hot sauce
Lime Crema (page 52)
Fresh basil, chopped

1 avocado, sliced
1 lime, cut into wedges

Wraps:
8 corn tortillas (or 8 large
  lettuce leaves)

HOW TO

Prepare your selected fillings and fixings.

Preheat the oven to 350°F. If you have a gas stovetop, wrap the tortillas in aluminum foil and use metal tongs to heat them directly over the flame for 1 to 2 minutes per side. Otherwise, in a pan over medium-low heat, fry the tortillas, one at a time, for 1 to 2 minutes per side then wrap them in foil. Keep the tortillas warm in the oven until you're ready to serve.

Assembling your tacos is different for everyone—start with the protein and layer on different fixings to create a unique finished product. Sometimes, I like to break up the tortillas and make a heaping taco salad.

COOK'S NOTE

*The pickled onions and slaw can be doubled up and left in their marinade
in the fridge for an extra day or two and served with grilled chicken,
a burger, or a salad another night. Corn tortillas give a more authentic flavour.
They are small, so you need 2 to 3 per person. Flour tortillas are another
great option; they are bigger, so you only need 1 or 2.*

ROASTED CAULIFLOWER

This is what you call a versatile dish. It's a fantastic taco filling, but you can also enjoy it as a side or even a main.

MAKES ENOUGH FOR 8 TACOS (OR SERVES 2 TO 4 AS A SIDE DISH)

INGREDIENTS

½ large head cauliflower, cut into small florets

3 Tbsp olive oil

1 Tbsp chopped sage

1 tsp ground cumin, or to taste

½ tsp chili powder, or to taste

Salt + freshly cracked pepper

¼ cup grated Gruyère (optional)

HOW TO

Preheat the oven to 450°F. Line a baking sheet with parchment paper. Arrange the cauliflower florets on the prepared baking sheet. Drizzle with the oil, and sprinkle with the sage, cumin, chili powder, and salt and pepper. Toss to coat.

Roast for 15 minutes, or until the florets are dark brown and crispy on the bottom. Flip them and sprinkle the Gruyère overtop (if using). Continue roasting until the florets are soft and golden and a bit shrivelled up, about 15 to 20 minutes.

COOK'S NOTE

Try adding 8 whole shishito peppers to the baking sheet with the cauliflower and roast for 15 minutes or more until they soften and shrivel. Once roasted, pull out their stems and discard, then rough-chop and stir the shisitos into the cauliflower to incorporate for some added heat and flavour. Top with 1 lb/455 g of crispy fried pancetta, broken into pieces, to make this into a more substantial meal.

CHILI-LIME SHRIMP WITH CORN SUCCOTASH

This taco filling also makes a perfect light supper on its own. Or you can load it up with black beans and guacamole as a more substantial bowl for dinner.

MAKES ENOUGH FOR 8 TACOS

INGREDIENTS

1 lb/455 g shrimp, thawed, peeled, deveined + patted dry (about 16 to 20 large, or 26 to 30 medium-size shrimp)

Marinade:

4 cloves garlic, minced

2 tsp smoked paprika

1 tsp ground cumin

1 tsp chili powder

½ tsp cayenne

½ tsp fine sea salt

½ tsp freshly ground pepper

Juice of 2 limes

¼ cup olive oil

2 Tbsp honey

Succotash:

2 Tbsp vegetable oil

½ to 1 jalapeno, or to taste, minced

4 green onions, white + light green parts only, sliced

1 red bell pepper, diced

1 cup fresh or frozen corn, thawed

HOW TO

In a large bowl, combine all the marinade ingredients. Add the shrimp and toss to thoroughly coat. Cover and marinate in the fridge for 15 to 30 minutes.

For the succotash, in a sauté pan over medium-high heat, heat the oil. Add the jalapeno and fry for 1 minute. Add the onions and bell peppers and fry for 1 to 2 minutes. Add the shrimp and fry for about 1 minute, until the undersides are opaque and pinkish. Flip the shrimp, add the corn, and sauté for 2 to 3 minutes, or until the shrimp are pink and cooked through.

LEMON WHITE FISH

This simple fish taco filling can also be a kid-friendly quick, midweek main when paired with a healthy side like sautéed rainbow chard (page 142).

MAKES ENOUGH FOR 8 TACOS

INGREDIENTS

1½ lb/680 g skinless flaky white fish (haddock, cod + tilapia are all good)

½ tsp chili flakes

½ tsp chili powder

Salt + freshly cracked pepper

1 Tbsp butter, for frying

1 Tbsp grapeseed oil, for frying

Zest + juice of 1 lemon

2 Tbsp chopped herbs (like chives + parsley)

HOW TO

Season the fish with the chili flakes, chili powder, and salt and pepper, coating both sides.

If you're frying, in a large nonstick pan over medium-high heat, melt the butter with the oil, swirling the pan to ensure the butter doesn't burn. Add the fish and fry for 2 to 3 minutes on one side. Add the lemon zest and juice, and flip the fish. Scatter the fresh herbs on top and cook for another 2 to 3 minutes, or until the fish is just cooked and golden in colour.

If you're barbecuing, wrap the seasoned fish with the fresh herbs, lemon zest, and juice in foil and barbecue on medium-high heat for 6 to 8 minutes (about 7 minutes per inch) or until just cooked through. Break the fish into large chunks for tacos.

COOK'S NOTE

If you want to add some crunch, after seasoning the fish, dip it into lemon juice, then coat it in a mixture of panko breadcrumbs and grated Parmesan, and fry per the method above. If you feel like splurging, you can also substitute black cod and marinate it in a tablespoon of miso for 30 minutes or so before frying. This is another good recipe to teach your teens to add to their recipe arsenal.

GRILLED FLANK STEAK

This is another family favourite. Charlotte calls it "bead" steak because the softened peppercorns look like beads. She agrees those beads add great flavour, which is funny for a girl who doesn't like pepper. I use this simple steak as a taco filling or you can also serve it as the main event alongside one or more of the sides on pages 128 to 161. (Note the steak should marinate for at least 24 hours.)

MAKES ENOUGH FOR 8 TACOS

INGREDIENTS

1½ to 2 lb/680 to 900 g flank
  steak

Marinade:
¼ cup red wine
¼ cup olive oil

¼ cup soy sauce
1 Tbsp sweet chili sauce
  (optional)
2 Tbsp whole peppercorns
1 Tbsp minced ginger

HOW TO

If the flank steak isn't scored (the butcher now usually does it for you), score it crosswise against the grain.

For the marinade, combine the ingredients in a measuring cup. Place the steak in a sealable plastic bag or dish and pour in the marinade. Marinate, sealed or covered, in the fridge for at least 24 hours, but no longer than 48 hours, turning occasionally.

At least 15 minutes before grilling, remove the steak from the fridge, bring to room temperature, and discard the marinade just before cooking.

Meanwhile, preheat the barbecue to high heat or an indoor grill pan over medium-high heat. Grill the steak to your desired doneness (for medium-rare, 5 to 7 minutes per side). Let the steak rest for 10 minutes at room temperature. Slice very thinly against the grain.

MAINS
Fish + Seafood, Chicken + Meat

Fish + Seafood

Chicken

Meat

BBQ MAPLE TROUT + SWISS CHARD

I never loved fish until I started buying local trout from Kolapore Springs. It is fresh and mild, and everyone, even fish skeptics like me, loves it. And it only takes a few minutes to roast or grill.

SERVES 4

INGREDIENTS

2 Tbsp soy sauce

3 Tbsp maple syrup

1 Tbsp olive oil

1 lemon, halved

2 tsp Dijon mustard

½ tsp chili flakes

Salt + freshly cracked pepper

2 small sides local trout

1 bunch Swiss chard or broccolini

2 cloves garlic, minced

HOW TO

In a small bowl, whisk together the soy sauce, maple syrup, oil, juice from half a lemon, mustard, and chili flakes, and season with salt and pepper.

Line a baking sheet with aluminum foil. Place the trout side by side on the foil. Pour the marinade overtop and flip the fish to coat. Seal the foil and let the fish marinate in the fridge for at least 30 minutes and up to a few hours.

Preheat the barbecue to high. Open the foil and lay the chard on top of the fish, followed by the garlic and a squirt of lemon juice. Seal the foil again and grill the trout for about 10 minutes until just cooked through and not translucent (8 minutes per inch of thickness.)

COOK'S NOTE

If you don't like fully steamed greens, grill the chard or broccolini instead with a bit of olive oil directly on the grill.

CARAMELIZED STICKY SALMON

My friend Ghislaine converted Fin to being a fish lover with this salmon. It has a winning combination of flavours, and the maple syrup creates an almost candied crust. It's best to marinate the fish for 24 hours before you plan to eat it if you can.

SERVES 4

INGREDIENTS

¼ cup soy sauce

¼ cup butter

¼ cup maple syrup or packed brown sugar

2 cloves garlic

1 Tbsp grated ginger (optional)

4 (6 to 8 oz/175 to 225 g each) centre-cut salmon fillets

Freshly cracked pepper

HOW TO

In a small pot over medium heat, combine the soy sauce, butter, maple syrup, and garlic. Cook for a few minutes, whisking, until thickened. Add in the ginger (if using). Set aside to cool.

Place the salmon in a shallow dish and pour the marinade over it. Season with pepper.

Cover and marinate in the fridge for 30 minutes, or up to 24 hours, turning occasionally.

Preheat the oven to 425°F. Line a baking sheet with parchment paper. Remove the fish from the marinade and place it on the prepared sheet. Bake for about 8 to 10 minutes (8 minutes per inch of thickness), or until the fish is just cooked with a little pink in the middle.

COOK'S NOTE

You can also cook the fish in a nonstick pan over medium-high heat for about 5 minutes per side. For an added salty tang, add 1 to 2 tablespoons of miso paste to the marinade. Try doubling this recipe and freezing the extra raw fish, in the marinade, in a resealable plastic bag. Before cooking, thaw to room temperature, remove the excess marinade, and bake as above. Serve with Yamato-Style Veggie Fried Rice (page 149).

BBQ Maple Trout + Swiss Chard, page 202

SHRIMP COCONUT GREEN CURRY

This is a great midweek kitchen counter dinner for two. It uses common pantry, fridge, and freezer items, making it easy to whip up. It's also a great catch-all base for whatever vegetables you have on hand. Experiment with the heat by trying milder red or yellow Thai curry paste instead of the green. You can cook this in the time it takes for rice to cook.

SERVES 2

INGREDIENTS

2 tsp coconut oil or vegetable oil

1 tsp vegetable oil

½ sweet onion, cut into small dice

½ jalapeno or 1 small chili pepper, seeds removed, minced

2 to 3 tsp Thai green curry paste

1 (14 oz/400 g) bag tiger shrimp, thawed, peeled, deveined + patted dry

½ red bell pepper, thinly sliced

1 (14 oz/398 ml) can coconut milk

1 cup frozen baby peas or shelled edamame, thawed

1 cup frozen corn kernels (optional)

Salt + freshly cracked pepper

Juice of 1 lime

2 green onions, white + light green parts only, thinly sliced

½ bunch basil, chiffonade

2 cups cooked rice, for serving

HOW TO

In a large sauté pan over medium heat, heat both oils. Add the onions and sauté until softened, a few minutes. Add the jalapeno and fry for a minute or two. Slowly and carefully stir in the curry paste. It sputters and burns easily. Fry for another minute. Add the shrimp and quickly fry each side until they start to turn pink, just a few minutes per side. Add the peppers and sauté for 1 minute.

Stir in the coconut milk, increase the heat to high, and bring to a low boil. Boil for a few minutes without stirring. Mix in the peas and corn (if using), and boil for another few minutes until cooked through. Remove from the heat.

Season with salt and pepper, and mix in the lime juice. Top with the green onions and basil. Enjoy over your favourite steaming hot rice.

COOK'S NOTE

*To switch this up, use 1 lb/455 g of sliced raw chicken in place of the shrimp,
and fry for about 10 minutes; try other vegetables like broccoli; add more
heat with more jalapeno; or substitute the rice with vermicelli noodles,
add them to the curry along with the peas and corn to soften.*

CLASSIC ROAST CHICKEN

We make this roast chicken a once-a-week ritual. It's so easy. And it makes great leftovers for the next day. Hello, roast chicken sandwich. My mom makes gravy for this. I don't … Instead, I spoon the drippings on top while it cooks for a crunchy outside and tender inside, and then drizzle again over the cooked chicken just before serving. Serve this with one of the carrot sides (pages 138 to 141), or throw some carrots in to roast alongside it, and you'll be transported back to childhood.

SERVES 4

INGREDIENTS

1 tsp butter + 2 Tbsp butter, cubed

1 (about 4 to 5 lb/1.8 to 2.2 kg) roasting chicken

Salt + freshly cracked pepper

1 lemon, halved

1 sweet onion, cut into wedges

2 stalks celery, tops, leaves + stalks roughly chopped

3 sprigs thyme

HOW TO

Preheat the oven to 375°F. Grease the bottom of a large roasting pan or large cast-iron pan or Dutch oven with the 1 teaspoon of butter.

Season the chicken's cavity with salt and pepper. Place the lemon halves in each side of the cavity with one of the onion wedges and celery leaves. Top the chicken with the cubes of butter, and the thyme, and season with salt and pepper. Place the chicken in the prepared pan.

Roast, uncovered, for 45 minutes, basting several times. Remove from the oven.

Arrange the celery and remaining onion wedges around the chicken. Return to the oven and cook for 45 minutes more, or until cooked through—the juices will run clear and a thermometer inserted into the thickest part will reach 170°F. Let the chicken rest at room temperature for 10 to 15 minutes.

To serve, use a slotted spoon to scoop the celery and onions into a small serving dish. Cut the wings and legs from the chicken. Remove the breast meat and slice. Top with the drippings (where all the flavour and, yes, the fat are).

SHAKE + BAKE LEMON CHICKEN

My friend Tori's mother-in-law, Libby, is a great cook, used to feeding her large extended family and often other regulars. This is one of her classics: a great make-ahead meal that's ideal for crowds. It's her iteration of a classic old recipe from the 70s—you know, the best kind, the ones that are shared within a community and change with the times (the original recipe had twice as many lemons, and no greens). It is perfect with asparagus and a simple salad. (Note this has to marinate overnight.)

SERVES 6

INGREDIENTS

6 boneless, skinless chicken breasts

Juice of 6 lemons

1 cup all-purpose flour

2 tsp paprika

1 tsp salt

Freshly cracked pepper

¼ cup vegetable oil

⅓ cup packed brown sugar

Zest of 1 lemon

½ cup chicken stock

2 lemons, sliced

2 Tbsp butter

6 cups baby spinach

2 Tbsp chopped flat-leaf parsley

HOW TO

Using a meat tenderizer, pound the chicken to flatten it slightly and evenly. Place the chicken and lemon juice in a large resealable bag or casserole dish with a lid. Marinate in the fridge overnight, turning once.

Preheat the oven to 350°F. Remove the chicken from the marinade. Place the flour, paprika, salt, and some pepper in a plastic bag and shake to combine, or combine the ingredients together on a plate. Add the chicken, one breast at a time, and toss to coat.

In a large fry pan over medium-high heat, heat half of the oil. Working in batches, fry each piece of chicken until browned, about 2 to 3 minutes per side, adding more oil as needed.

Transfer the chicken to a large baking dish with a bit of space between them. Sprinkle with the sugar and lemon zest, cover with the stock, top with the lemon slices, and bake for 20 minutes until cooked through.

In a large fry pan over medium heat, melt the butter. Add the spinach and use tongs to toss.

Cook until warmed, about 2 minutes. Top the chicken with the buttered spinach and the parsley. Serve immediately.

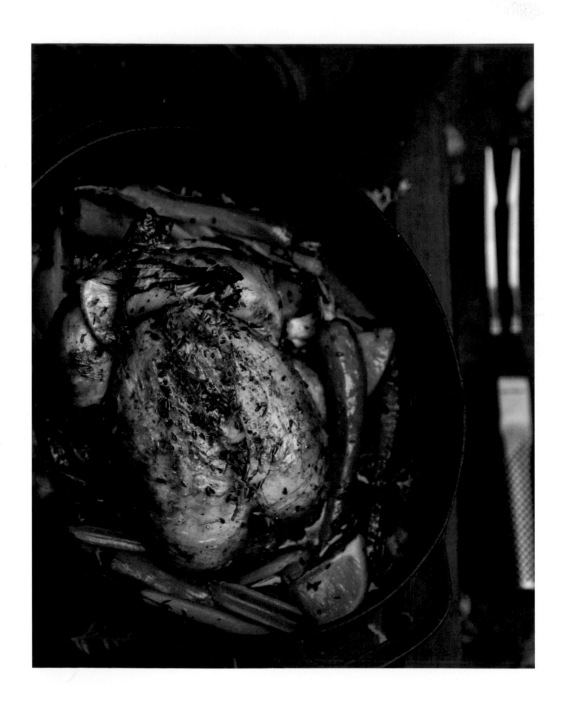

Classic Roast Chicken, page 208

MAMMA MIA CHICKEN

My sister-in-law Amy and brother Jeff shared their family-favourite chicken recipe with us: a "pizza chicken" baked with basil, tomatoes, and mozzarella. The recipe was from Melissa Clark's *Dinner: Changing the Game*. When I was creating my own version, I added capers and olives for a Mediterranean spin. My mom tested it on my brother Tim and his wife Nancy and their family, and finally, after many adjustments, we nailed it. If I were running a fabulous *Mamma Mia*–style inn in Greece, this would be the house signature dish.

SERVES 4

INGREDIENTS

8 bone-in, skin-on chicken thighs

2 tsp fine sea salt

Freshly cracked pepper

1 Tbsp olive oil

2 cloves garlic, minced

1 shallot, or ½ small sweet onion, finely diced

½ to ¾ cup pitted + halved Niçoise olives

1 to 2 Tbsp capers, drained (optional)

½ tsp chili flakes

¼ cup white wine

1 (28 oz/796 ml) can San Marzano tomatoes

1 pint cherry tomatoes

½ cup basil, chiffonade

8 oz/225 g mozzarella, thinly sliced with Y-peeler

HOW TO

Preheat the oven to 400°F. Pat the chicken dry and season with half of the salt and generous amounts of pepper.

In a large cast-iron skillet or large fry pan, heat the olive oil. Brown the chicken, in batches if necessary, and sear on all sides until just browned, about 10 minutes. Remove the chicken from the pan and set aside.

To the same pan, add the garlic, shallots, olives, capers, and chili flakes, and sauté for 1 minute. Deglaze the pan with the white wine. Stir in the canned tomatoes with their juice.

Use a wooden spoon to break them up. Add the cherry tomatoes. Season with the remaining salt and some pepper and add ¼ cup of the basil. Cook for about 10 minutes, breaking up the tomatoes, until chunky.

Return the chicken to the cast-iron skillet; if you aren't using a cast-iron skillet, transfer it to a casserole dish. Bake, uncovered, for 40 minutes, or until the juices run clear. Top with the remaining basil and cover with the mozzarella in a single layer. Turn the oven to broil and broil for 3 minutes or until the cheese bubbles and oozes.

CURRIED CHICKEN THIGHS WITH POMEGRANATE

Curry powder is the workhorse of the spice world: as a blend of many spices, it does the work for us. The combination of the aromas of the curry combined with the crunch of pomegranate seeds will have you coming back to this one time and time again. Enjoy this with your favourite winter salad (like the Christmas Euchre Tourney Salad on page 96), or with Simple Toasts (page 51), or over rice.

SERVES 4

INGREDIENTS

8 boneless, skinless chicken thighs

Salt + freshly cracked pepper

2 Tbsp coconut or vegetable oil

2 tsp curry powder

1 cup chicken stock

½ cup plain yogurt or sour cream

1 cup pomegranate seeds

4 cups cooked rice, for serving

HOW TO

Pat dry the chicken, and season with salt and pepper.

In a large fry pan over medium heat, heat the oil. Add the curry powder and fry for 1 minute, stirring with a wooden spoon. For a deeper curry flavour and more heat, use an additional teaspoon or two of curry powder. Add the chicken. Increase the heat to medium-high and fry the chicken until browned, about 3 minutes per side, cooking in batches if needed. Remove the chicken and set aside.

To the same pan, add the stock to the pan and bring to a boil over medium-high heat, scraping the bottom of the pan to incorporate any bits of chicken that got stuck, and reduce until thickened, about 5 minutes. Turn down the heat to medium. Return the chicken to the pan. Cook until the chicken juices run clear, about 15 minutes.

In the pan, top the chicken with the yogurt, allowing it to warm and run down into the sauce. Remove from the heat, and top with the pomegranate seeds. Enjoy over rice.

SOUTHERN-BAKED CHICKEN WITH HONEY BUTTER

I never understood the classic Southern combo of chicken and waffles, or having something sweet with chicken. But I am a professed sweet tooth who was spoiled by my dad's maple syrup and honey, and I also have kids who would default to breaded chicken fingers given the chance, so this recipe was born. It's oven-baked, but it gives fried chicken a run for its money. And it travels well, so try this for your next outdoor gathering or ski lunch.

SERVES 4

INGREDIENTS

½ cup all-purpose flour

1 egg

1 cup buttermilk

Salt + freshly cracked pepper

1½ cups panko breadcrumbs

2 sprigs thyme, leaves only

1 tsp paprika

½ tsp cayenne

8 small boneless, skinless chicken thighs

1 head broccoli, cut into florets

6 Tbsp butter

2 Tbsp honey

HOW TO

Preheat the oven to 450°F. Line a baking sheet with parchment paper.

Prepare a dredging station: Put the flour on a plate. In a bowl, whisk the egg and buttermilk with salt and pepper. In a second bowl, combine the panko breadcrumbs with the thyme, paprika, cayenne, and salt and pepper. Season the chicken on all sides with salt and pepper.

One piece at a time, coat the chicken in the flour, dip in the egg mixture, shaking off any excess, dip in the breadcrumb mixture, and place on the prepared baking sheet.

Bake for 20 minutes, flipping halfway through, until cooked through and brown on top.

In a medium pot over high heat, blanch the broccoli in boiling salted water until the stems are just tender and bright green, about 2 minutes. Do not overcook. Set aside.

In a small pot over medium heat, bring the butter and honey to a boil and boil, stirring, for 1 minute.

Remove the chicken from the oven and add the broccoli to the baking sheet. Bake for another few minutes, until the chicken is browned and the broccoli softened. Drizzle the butter-honey sauce over the chicken and broccoli and serve.

COOK'S NOTE

If you don't have buttermilk, just use 2 eggs instead, or add 1 tablespoon of white vinegar to the milk.
If you like more heat, you can add chili flakes, to the breadcrumb mixture or serve with your
favourite hot sauce. Feel free to swap the broccoli for another vegetable.

THAI-STYLE CHICKEN LETTUCE WRAPS

Step aside, beef taco kit. These lettuce wraps are healthier and more delicious. Once you try these, your Tuesday Taco night will be forever upgraded.

INGREDIENTS

3 Tbsp vegetable oil

½ red onion, cut into small dice

8 oz/225 g cremini mushrooms, trimmed, cleaned + cut into small dice

2 lb/900 g ground chicken

¼ cup Thai sweet chili sauce

¼ cup hoisin sauce

¼ cup soy sauce

2 Tbsp sriracha or hot sauce of your choice

2 Tbsp rice wine vinegar

1 Tbsp minced ginger

1 red or yellow bell pepper, cut into small dice

4 cups baby spinach

½ cup chopped basil

6 green onions, white + light green parts only, thinly sliced

Zest + juice of 1 lime

2 carrots, grated, for garnish (optional)

1 lime, cut into wedges, for garnish

2 heads Bibb lettuce or romaine hearts, leaves separated

HOW TO

In a large sauté pan over medium heat, heat the oil. Add the onions and sauté until translucent, about 5 minutes.

Add the mushrooms and sauté for a minute. Add the chicken and cook until browned and cooked through, about 10 minutes.

In a small bowl, combine the chili sauce, hoisin sauce, soy sauce, sriracha, rice vinegar, and ginger.

Add the sauce and the bell peppers to the chicken mixture, stirring to combine. Simmer until the sauce is reduced and thickened, about 3 to 4 minutes. Add the spinach, turn off the heat, and toss to incorporate. Stir in the basil and green onions, followed by the lime zest and juice.

Transfer to a bowl. Place the carrots and lime wedges in separate small bowls and arrange the lettuce leaves on a platter. Serve family-style.

Add ½ cup chopped peanuts or cashews as a nice additional topping.

ODE TO THE BARBECUE

I love to barbecue in all four seasons. Sometimes I find it easier than using the oven since you can see and touch the ingredients, and there's peace and kind of an escape in being outside. In our family, the best straw to draw is the one for grill duty, for the fun ritual of gathering around the grill (in the summertime anyway). Whether you have a little hibachi, a charcoal homemade grill like my dad's at the cottage, or a full bells and whistles setup, there are a few things to remember.

Make sure you have a good-quality cleaning brush for scrubbing pre- and post-grilling, long-handled tongs, and a flipper. Double-check your propane, if that's your fuel of choice, and for safety make sure that the lid

is up before you light the grill. Give it time to preheat. Once it's hot, brush it clean. Be sure to bring your meat to room temperature before hitting the grill to maximize tenderness. Barbecue according to the recipe. When done, place the meat on a fresh platter or board and let it rest for 10 minutes: be patient, and let the juices recess to give you maximum flavour and tenderness before you carve; remember, meat continues to cook off the grill.

Ensure you turn everything off when you're done. And don't forget to clean the fat-catch dish underneath regularly. Oh yes, and enjoy the moment, maybe with a drink in hand, and hopefully good company.

MUSTARD-MAPLE PORK CHOPS

The source and quality matter a lot with pork—and all other meat, of course. For this recipe, visit your favourite butcher for good-quality, pasture-raised pork chops that have come from a small farm and named producer to ensure the best quality, flavour, tenderness, and yes, fat. On the bone is best for tenderness and flavour. Our local butchers, Olliffe and Cumbrae's, both carry Tamworth pork from Perth County, apparently the best heritage pork in Ontario. Enjoy these chops with sweet potato fries (page 158).

SERVES 4

INGREDIENTS

Pork:

2 Tbsp extra-grainy Dijon mustard

2 Tbsp maple syrup

1 Tbsp olive oil

½ tsp chili powder

Salt + freshly cracked pepper

4 (1 inch thick or more) pork loins or T-bone chops, on the bone

Apples:

2 Tbsp melted butter

2 Tbsp brown sugar

1 Tbsp honey

2 tsp ground cinnamon

3 Granny Smith apples, peeled, cored + sliced into wedges

HOW TO

Preheat the barbecue to medium-high heat.

For the pork, in a bowl, combine the mustard, maple syrup, oil, chili powder, and salt and pepper. Rub the mustard-maple mixture all over the pork chops.

For the apples, in a bowl, mix together the butter, sugar, honey, and cinnamon. Add the apples and toss to thoroughly coat.

Sear the chops for 3 to 5 minutes per side until they have a nice crust and sear marks. Turn down the heat to medium, close the lid, and cook for another 5 minutes or so until the pork reaches 150°F on a meat thermometer and is no longer pink. While the pork is grilling, place the apples directly on the grill, and grill until there are grill marks. Move to the cooler side of the grill and cook until soft, about 5 minutes. Let the pork rest for 5 minutes before serving.

BBQ STICKY RIBS

Our local grocery, Summerhill Market, has ribs marinated and ready for us to just throw on the grill. They are my guilty pleasure. But memories of my aunt Nancy's ribs remind me it's worth the effort to prepare them myself. These are sticky and messy and delicious. Extra napkins are required. (Note these are best marinated in the fridge overnight or for the day.) Enjoy with the best of corn in season and some Taco Slaw (page 87).

SERVES 4 TO 6

INGREDIENTS

1 cup barbecue sauce

¼ cup ketchup

2 Tbsp soy sauce

2 Tbsp miso paste (optional)

2 Tbsp honey

2 Tbsp olive oil

2 Tbsp brown sugar

3 slab sides (about 4 to 5 lb/1.8 to 2.2 kg in total) baby back ribs

HOW TO

In a bowl, mix together the barbecue sauce, ketchup, soy sauce, miso paste, honey, olive oil, and sugar. Place the ribs in a roasting pan (lined with aluminum foil for easy cleaning) and pour the marinade overtop. Turn the ribs to coat them evenly in the marinade, cover the pan with aluminum foil, and marinate in the fridge overnight or for a minimum of 8 hours.

Remove the ribs from the fridge an hour before you want to cook them to bring them to room temperature. Preheat the oven to 325°F.

Roast the ribs, still covered, for 1½ hours. Increase the heat to 400°F and roast for another 45 minutes or until the ribs are very tender and starting to fall off the bone.

KOREAN BEEF SHORT RIBS

This is another of my quick-grill family favourites. These take no time on the barbecue, so be sure your sides are ready to go. They're equally good cold the next day, and great for a picnic. Devour these with a baked potato and Taco Slaw (page 87). (Note these need to marinate in the fridge for at least 12 hours.)

SERVES 4

INGREDIENTS

½ cup honey

½ cup soy sauce

⅓ cup sake or rice wine vinegar

1 Tbsp sambal oelek or hot chili sauce

1 Tbsp grated ginger

3 lb/1.4 kg (very thin) sides Korean or Miami ribs (3 or 4 sides per person)

HOW TO

In a shallow dish, combine the honey, soy sauce, sake, sambal oelek, and ginger. Add the ribs, tossing to ensure they are covered in the marinade. Marinate, covered, in the fridge for at least 12 hours, or up to 24 hours, flipping once.

Remove the ribs from the fridge 30 minutes before you want to cook them to bring them to room temperature. Preheat the barbecue to high heat. Discard the marinade.

Grill the ribs for 3 to 4 minutes per side, until the ribs are seared and just cooked through.

FRIDAY NIGHT BURGERS

Over the years, Friday nights would find us on the road looking forward to my mom's famous burgers. We would descend upon Four Wheel Farm, often in a snowstorm, and as the fire was roaring, wine bottles were opened and burgers were grilling. It was hard to grow up and leave the nest. As middle-aged adults, with our own kids, we still come back often, usually at meal time. When I met Peter, I learned he made burgers—a risky comparison. Peter uses lean ground beef; my mom uses medium-lean. He adds heat with jalapenos, onions, and horse-radish. Mom caramelizes onions in a cast-iron pan, ditches the jalapenos, and serves her burgers with slaw and chips. Whichever we choose, we have great Friday night burgers. Added bonus, I'm not the one making them—cook's night off.

MAKES 6

INGREDIENTS

Patties:

2½ to 3 lb/1.1 to 1.4 kg lean or medium-lean ground beef

2 eggs

¼ large sweet Vidalia onion, cut into small dice

1 jalapeno, stem and seeds removed, minced

2 Tbsp ketchup

2 Tbsp yellow mustard

2 Tbsp Worcestershire

1 tsp horseradish

2 tsp fine sea salt

Freshly cracked pepper

Fixing Options:

6 buns

6 to 12 slices cheddar

Fried bacon

Harissa

Ketchup, mustard, relish

Pickled Jalapenos (page 42)

Lettuce

Mushrooms, sautéed

Onions, caramelized

Tomato slices

HOW TO

In a large bowl, use your hands to begin to break up the ground beef. Add the eggs, onions, jalapeno, ketchup, mustard, Worcestershire, horseradish, salt, and some pepper, and work the mixture together until incorporated. Form the mixture into 6 patties about 1½ inches thick. Set aside on a plate.

Preheat the barbecue to medium-high heat. Grill the patties about 5 to 7 minutes on one side until seared and charred. Flip and grill about 3 minutes more for medium-well. (Adjust the timings for your grill and desired doneness.)

In the last few minutes, place the buns on the top rack of the grill to toast them and top the patties with cheese slices (if using). Serve immediately with self-serve fixings bar.

GRILLED PEPPER STRIPLOINS WITH GREMOLATA

This classic recipe offers a fresh and seasonal combination of ingredients that needs little else except maybe some smashed potatoes (page 160) and grilled scallions to make it the perfect outdoor dinner. Top quality meat from a reputable butcher makes all the difference.

SERVES 4

INGREDIENTS

Striploins:

2 Tbsp Worcestershire sauce

1 Tbsp balsamic vinegar

1 Tbsp olive oil

2 tsp steak spice rub

Salt + freshly cracked pepper

2 (14 oz/400 g each) New York striploin steaks

Garden Herb Gremolata:

Zest of 1 lemon

2 cloves garlic, minced

½ cup finely chopped flat-leaf parsley

2 Tbsp finely chopped chives

Horseradish Mustard Sauce:

2 Tbsp plain yogurt

2 Tbsp prepared horseradish

1 Tbsp Dijon mustard

Salt + freshly cracked pepper

HOW TO

In a bowl, combine the Worcestershire, vinegar, oil, steak spice, and generous amounts of salt and pepper, and rub the steaks all over with it. Marinate, covered, for at least 1 hour in the fridge or up to 24 hours.

Preheat the barbecue to high heat. Remove the steaks from the fridge about 30 minutes before you plan to cook them to bring them to room temperature.

Grill the steaks for 5 minutes per side. Turn down the heat to medium, move the steaks to the cooler side of the grill, and grill to your desired doneness, 5 to 7 minutes for medium-rare. Let the steaks rest for 10 minutes before thinly slicing.

For the gremolata, in a small bowl using a fork, or with a mortar and pestle, combine the lemon, garlic, parsley, and chives, leaving the herbs chunky.

For the horseradish mustard sauce, in a small bowl, combine the yogurt, horseradish, mustard, and salt and pepper.

Serve the sliced steak with the gremolata and horseradish mustard sauce on the side.

COOK'S NOTE

The gremolata recipe can be doubled and used in sandwiches or pasta, or served alongside short ribs (page 226). For a little kick, add 1 minced jalapeno; for some crunch, add 2 tablespoons of chopped nuts of your choice. Extra gremolata can be stored in an airtight container in the fridge for a few days.

DESSERTS

BAKING ESSENTIALS

Here's the truth: I don't always love to cook. But I always love to bake. It's relaxing. And my girls find the same soothing calm from baking that I do.

You'll find my essential baking tools listed on page 37. I prefer to haul out the stand mixer for most baking, using either whisk or paddle attachments, but if you don't have one, a large bowl and hand mixer with beaters will work just fine. You can use a wooden spoon for many of the recipes—you'll just need a bit more muscle. When you're making meringues and whipping cream, though, electric is a must.

For best results, a note on a few simple techniques: "stirring" simply means incorporating ingredients together; whipping (or beating) means aerating on high speed; folding means mixing by lifting very carefully, with a light hand, to maintain a fluffy texture.

Like with cooking, using best-quality ingredients makes a difference to your baking results. Check the dates of your flours and spices to make sure they are fresh; you don't want to use ingredients that stayed over the winter at the cottage.

BUTTER

We are a salted butter family. It's our one-stop shop for spreading on toast, and for cooking and baking. Pastry chefs would not approve—they use unsalted butter and add salt separately for precision. If you have unsalted butter, just adjust the salt specified in the recipe.

EGGS

At chef school, the first thing we got tested on was eggs. You may think of eggs as humble and simple, but there are a few tricks that make all the difference: Crack your eggs on a flat surface, not the side of a bowl (counterintuitive, I know), and you'll get a much cleaner break. When separating lots of eggs (like for meringues), have a bowl for shells, a bowl for yolks, and a bowl for whites; note that cold eggs are easier to separate than eggs at room temperature. If you do get an egg yolk in the whites, use the shell to remove it. Also, room-temperature egg whites beat quicker than cold.

SUGAR

There are healthier, more natural options available to substitute for granulated sugar, like cane sugar, maple syrup, and honey. But, as a baker trained at a classic French chef school and by my mom and grandmother, I still use granulated in my baking recipes—they work perfectly and are delicious, albeit a little old-fashioned. When I was working with Mama Earth, the chefs and bakers created wonderful baked goods sweetened with fruits and unrefined sugars. Baking is a science, so note that it's not as simple as a cup-for-cup swap. But if you've mastered the art of using other sugar variations, swap away. For now, I'm an old dog continuing to learn new tricks.

OATMEAL CHOCOLATE CHIP COOKIES

A classic cookie. For the kids and the kid in you. Go ahead and eliminate the chocolate chips if you must (but it'll be a real shame).

MAKES 3 DOZEN COOKIES

INGREDIENTS

1 cup butter, room temperature

1 cup lightly packed brown sugar

¾ cup sugar

2 eggs

2 tsp pure vanilla extract

½ tsp fine sea salt

1 cup all-purpose flour

3 cups rolled oats

1 tsp baking soda

2 cups semisweet chocolate chips

HOW TO

Preheat the oven to 350°F.

In a stand mixer fitted with the paddle attachment, cream the butter with both sugars. Add the eggs, vanilla, and salt, and beat until smooth. Mix in the flour, oats, and baking soda until just combined, and then fold in the chocolate chips by hand.

Using a small cookie scoop, scoop the dough onto 2 ungreased baking sheets, 12 scoops per sheet (3 scoops across and 4 scoops down), leaving lots of equal space between each. Flatten each slightly.

Bake for 10 to 12 minutes, or until golden brown. Let rest on the sheets for 2 minutes, then transfer to a cooling rack to cool completely. Repeat with the remaining dough for 1 more sheet of 12 cookies. You can store the cookies in a cookie tin for a day or two, or until they disappear.

COOK'S NOTE

To grease or not to grease your baking pans: For cookies, there's enough fat in the mixture that you don't need to grease the sheets, despite most old recipes calling to grease. My sister-in-law Amanda's cookies really are the best, and she greases the pan, but I don't, so I guess the verdict is still out.

BUTTERSCOTCH + CHOCOLATE CHUNK COOKIES

It was hard to come up with any cookie better than the classic chocolate chip cookie my extended family has perfected (see the Chocolate Chip Cookie Ice-Cream Sandwiches on page 242). And then I remembered butterscotch chips from my childhood. And from my old favourite store-bought Cookie It Up shortbread that uses chocolate chunks instead of chocolate chips. Together they're a killer combo. Olivia tested this more than any other recipe in this book. Not that we needed to . . .

MAKES 4 DOZEN COOKIES

INGREDIENTS

1 cup butter, room temperature

1⅓ cups lightly packed brown sugar

½ cup sugar

2 eggs

2 tsp pure vanilla extract

2 cups all-purpose flour

1 tsp baking soda

1 tsp fine sea salt

¾ cup butterscotch chips

2 cups dark chocolate chips (or 48 small chunk pieces)

HOW TO

Preheat the oven to 350°F.

In a stand mixer fitted with the paddle attachment, cream the butter and both sugars until light and fluffy. Add the eggs one at a time, beating well after each addition. Mix in the vanilla, and then the flour, baking soda, and salt until just combined. Do not overmix. Fold in the butterscotch and dark chocolate chips by hand (if you're using chocolate chunks rather than chips, fold in just the butterscotch chips at this time).

Using a small cookie scoop or 2 spoons, scoop the dough onto 2 ungreased baking sheets, 12 scoops per sheet (3 scoops across and 4 scoops down), leaving lots of equal space between each. If using chocolate chunks, press 1 chunk into the top of each cookie using your thumb.

Bake for 8 minutes or until the cookies are light golden and soft. Let rest on the sheets for 2 minutes, then transfer to a cooling rack to cool completely. Repeat with the remaining dough for 2 more sheets of 12 cookies each. You can store extra cookies in a cookie tin for a few days, if they can last that long.

COOK'S NOTE

For a pretty and professional-looking variation, instead of
folding in the chocolate chips, press a single chocolate chunk into the
top of each cookie. If you're thinking about swapping chocolates, know that
semisweet has the least amount of cacao so will pack the least punch,
and bittersweet has a more intense flavour.

CHOCOLATE CHIP COOKIE ICE-CREAM SANDWICHES

The recipe for these cookies originated from *The Cottage Cookbook*, the beloved and still much-used community cookbook put together by my mom's generation of our cottage community. We tweaked this recipe to perfection over two summers, and now Liv knows the recipe by heart, and Charlotte makes them perfectly, although they now sometimes make them for the dough only (so bad, I know). These cookies have become the base for the best ice-cream sandwich ever. Make as many ice-cream sandwiches as you need in the moment, and freeze the remaining cookies to eat solo, or with ice cream another day (and see how long they last).

MAKES 48 COOKIES (ENOUGH FOR 24 ICE-CREAM SANDWICHES)

INGREDIENTS

- 1 cup butter, room temperature
- 1 cup packed brown sugar
- 1 cup sugar
- 2 eggs

- 2 tsp pure vanilla extract
- 2 cups all-purpose flour
- 1 tsp baking soda
- 1 tsp fine sea salt

- 2 cups semisweet chocolate chips
- 1 scoop chocolate or vanilla ice cream per sandwich (I like Miller's and Kawartha Dairy)

HOW TO

Preheat the oven to 350°F.

In a stand mixer fitted with the paddle attachment, cream the butter and both sugars until light and fluffy. Add the eggs and vanilla and beat well. Mix in the flour, baking soda, and salt until just combined. Fold in the chocolate chips by hand.

Using a small cookie scoop or 2 spoons, scoop the dough onto 2 ungreased baking sheets, 12 scoops per sheet (3 scoops across and 4 scoops down), leaving lots of space between each cookie. Ever so slightly flatten each cookie.

Bake for 7 to 8 minutes or until light golden but soft. Let rest on the sheets for 2 minutes, then transfer to a cooling rack to cool completely. Repeat with the remaining dough for 2 more sheets of 12 cookies each. Store extra cookies in a cookie tin for a day or two or until they disappear.

To make a cookie sandwich, take 1 cookie and top it with 1 scoop of ice cream. Place a second cookie on top and squish it down. If you want to make these ahead of time, wrap them individually in plastic and freeze until ready to serve.

LIV'S CHOCOLATE PUDDING

My grandmother's age-old chocolate pudding was a staple in our home when I was growing up. She made it with cocoa powder, and I published her recipe in my last cookbook, *In My Mother's Kitchen*. Then once, when Liv got a concussion, the only thing she felt up to doing was baking. The feel-good easy dessert she turned to was my grandma's somehow healing pudding. This recipe is the now-updated version, made richer by Liv's addition of chocolate chips.

SERVES 6 TO 8

INGREDIENTS

¼ cup sugar

¼ cup cornstarch

¼ tsp fine sea salt

4 cups milk

2 cups semisweet chocolate chips

Chocolate shavings, for garnish

HOW TO

In a heavy saucepan over medium heat, whisk together the sugar, cornstarch, salt, and milk. Whisk until it thickens and starts gently boiling, about 2 minutes. Remove from the heat. Stir in the chocolate chips until melted and incorporated. Pour into a glass bowl or individual ramekins. Refrigerate, covered with plastic wrap, for at least 3 hours and up to overnight to set. Garnish with chocolate shavings just before serving. Enjoy.

FUDGE BROWNIES

You can search all your life for true love. The search ends here. And the best part is you can all share and enjoy this one love together. Not for the faint of heart, but for the hard-core brownie lover.

MAKES 12 LARGE (OR 24 MINI) BROWNIES

INGREDIENTS

¾ cup butter, cold, cubed

6 oz/175 g unsweetened chocolate

4 eggs

2 cups sugar

1 Tbsp espresso powder or finely ground coffee

2½ tsp pure vanilla extract

1 cup all-purpose flour

½ tsp fine sea salt

1 cup semisweet chocolate chips

HOW TO

Preheat the oven to 350°F. Grease a 9- × 13-inch pan with butter and dust it with flour.

In a medium, heavy-bottomed pot over low heat, melt the butter and chocolate, stirring together. Once melted, set aside so it starts to cool.

In a large bowl, whisk together the eggs, sugar, coffee, and vanilla. Stir in the slightly cooled chocolate mixture. Fold in the flour and salt. Stir in the chocolate chips. Evenly spread the mixture into the prepared pan, smoothing out the top, and bake for 20 to 25 minutes or until set.

Let cool in the pan on a wire rack before cutting into 12 large or 24 mini brownies. Enjoy right away, or store wrapped in aluminum foil for a day or two.

COOK'S NOTE

Pastry chefs would have us melting chocolate in a bowl set over simmering water, ensuring no water touches the chocolate (see Kate's Dates on page 267). But, for this recipe, the fat in the butter means the chocolate won't seize so long as you melt them together over low heat. You can increase the chocolate chip amount or even add the whole bag—no one will complain.

CHOCOLATE CHIP ZUCCHINI LOAF

There's nothing like knowing there are vegetables in desserts that my kids love. When the kids first tested this, they asked if it was banana bread. My little white lie was "Sort of." After rave reviews, I laughed that they'd eaten zucchini vegetable dessert. The teen response was "You don't need to pull those stunts anymore, Mom." If you have picky eaters, know that the zucchini adds moisture, has very little flavour, and is grated so it's practically invisible. It's so moist and delicious, the word "zucchini" won't even come up.

MAKES TWO 5- × 9-INCH LOAVES

INGREDIENTS

1 cup vegetable oil

1 cup sugar

¾ cup lightly packed brown sugar

2 eggs

½ cup buttermilk

2 tsp pure vanilla extract

2 cups all-purpose flour

¼ cup cocoa

2 tsp ground cinnamon

1 tsp baking soda

½ tsp baking powder

½ tsp fine sea salt

1 cup semisweet chocolate chips

2 medium zucchinis, skin on, grated (about 2 cups)

HOW TO

Preheat the oven to 350°F. Grease two 5- × 9-inch loaf pans with butter.

In a stand mixer fitted with the paddle attachment, beat the oil and both sugars together. Add in the eggs, buttermilk, and vanilla, and beat well.

In a separate bowl, combine the flour, cocoa, cinnamon, baking soda, baking powder, and salt. Add the flour mixture to the stand mixer in 2 batches, and mix until just combined. Do not overmix. Fold in the chocolate chips and then the zucchini by hand. Divide the batter evenly between the 2 prepared loaf pans.

Bake for 50 to 55 minutes, until a toothpick inserted in the centre of a loaf comes out clean. In the final 10 minutes, if they are starting to really brown, cover them with aluminum foil to slow the browning. Cool in the pan on a wire rack. Once cool, run a knife around the edges and turn out on a rack to cool completely. Store, wrapped in parchment paper and then plastic wrap, at room temperature for up to 2 days, or in the freezer for up to 1 month.

COOK'S NOTE

You can use the largest side of a box grater if you want larger bits of zucchini. We didn't have loaf pans when we first tested this, and the recipe worked beautifully in a Bundt pan—it just required a slightly shorter cook time. If you don't have buttermilk, make your own by adding 1 teaspoon of vinegar or lemon juice to 1 cup of milk and letting it sit for a few minutes before using.

LEMON ANGEL CAKE

You know that delicious glossy light meringue you find on lemon meringue pie? You know that airy angel cake that makes you think you should have a second piece? I've combined them here and topped them with a perfect pucker of a classic lemon glaze. You've just met your new favourite cake for birthdays or any special occasions. My grandmother used to make a similar white cake to this for one of my aunt's birthdays on Christmas Eve, without the lemon, using peppermint instead. We are still in search of that recipe.

MAKES ONE 10-INCH ANGEL CAKE, SERVES 6 TO 8

INGREDIENTS

Cake:

2 cups sugar

1 cup all-purpose flour

8 egg whites

1 tsp cream of tartar

½ tsp fine sea salt

Zest of 2 lemons

2 Tbsp lemon juice

1 tsp pure vanilla extract

Lemon Glaze:

¼ cup lemon juice

1 cup icing sugar

For Serving:

Fresh berries or cooked Boozy Fruits (page 256) (optional)

Whipped cream (optional)

HOW TO

Preheat the oven to 325°F.

For the cake, sift 1 cup of the sugar and the flour into a large bowl. Sift again. Reserve.

In a stand mixer fitted with the whisk attachment, whip the egg whites on high speed until foamy. Add the cream of tartar and salt and whip until soft peaks form. Add the remaining sugar and whip until stiff, glossy peaks form. With the mixer running on low speed, add the lemon zest and juice and vanilla, and mix until just combined. Gently fold in the reserved flour-sugar mixture in 4 additions until incorporated.

Pour the batter into a 10-inch angel food pan. Smooth out the top. Bake for 35 to 40 minutes or until the cake pulls away from the sides of the pan and springs back when touched. Let cool completely in the pan.

To make the glaze, stir the lemon juice and icing sugar together until the sugar dissolves.

Slide a knife around the outside and inside perimeters of the pan. Invert the cake on a platter. Drizzle the glaze over the cake, and serve with fresh whipped cream and berries. Store leftover cake at room temperature for up to 2 days.

FROZEN LEMON POTS

I love to make desserts, but even though I'm a chef, I don't have an ice-cream maker. Who has the room? So this is cheater lemon ice cream. Quick and professional, it can be cottage-casual or party-fancy. It's all about how you present it. (Note this has to freeze overnight.)

SERVES 6

INGREDIENTS

1 cup 10% cream

1 cup whipping cream

⅔ cup sugar + 2 Tbsp to candy (optional)

Zest + juice of 2 lemons

1 lemon (optional), for garnish

HOW TO

In a stand mixer fitted with the paddle attachment, beat both creams on high speed until they thicken enough to coat the back of a spoon. Add the ⅔ cup of sugar and beat until incorporated and the consistency resembles whipped cream. Do not overbeat. Fold in the lemon zest and juice.

Place 6 small 3- to 4-inch freezer-proof ramekins on a tray. Divide the mixture evenly between them. Cover each tightly with aluminum foil and freeze until firm, at least 8 hours or overnight.

To make a candied lemon garnish, use a Y-peeler to peel the lemon rind only (avoiding the white bitter pith) into 6 long strips. Place the remaining 2 tablespoons of sugar in a small bowl, dip the peels in the sugar to coat, and place on a baking sheet. Freeze overnight.

To serve, garnish the lemon pots with the candied lemon.

STRAWBERRY RHUBARB FOOL

A fool is an English dessert. I'm drawn to the name. Traditionally, you simply fold stewed fruit into whipped cream. It makes for the perfect quick dessert when you have extra whipping cream on hand.

SERVES 4

INGREDIENTS

¼ cup + 1 tsp maple syrup

Juice of 1 lemon (about ¼ cup)

4 stalks rhubarb, chopped

2 cups sliced strawberries

½ cup whipping cream

2 tsp pure vanilla extract

HOW TO

In a sauté pan over medium-high heat, warm the ¼ cup of maple syrup. Stir in the lemon juice and bring to a low boil. Add the rhubarb and simmer until soft, about 5 minutes. Add 1 cup of the strawberries and sauté for another 2 minutes until soft. Set aside to cool.

In a stand mixer fitted with the whisk attachment, whip the cream on high speed until soft peaks form. Add the remaining 1 teaspoon of maple syrup and the vanilla and whip on low speed to incorporate. Fold in the cooled fruit. Transfer to a glass bowl, or individual glass serving bowls, and chill in the fridge before serving. Serve with the remaining sliced strawberries.

COOK'S NOTE

You can make a self-serve fool bar by setting out pretty clear glasses, whipped cream, and cooked fruit and letting everyone assemble their own. As with any good bar, options are fun. Leave out lots of extra cut-up fresh fruit, crumbled cookies, or even jam. This makes a perfect side to the Lemon Angel Cake (page 250) for a pretty birthday party treat.

MERINGUE MESS WITH BOOZY FRUITS

My grandmother used to say meringues were best made on a sunny, clear day to get the perfect, dry result. If you attempt these on a humid or rainy day, consider yourself warned. These are best made the night before you plan to eat them—leave them in the oven after you've turned it off. The topping options are endless with these. Fresh whipped cream, seasonal berries, or your favourite boozy fruit compote. They are my ode to the traditional English Eton mess, and the satisfaction comes from turning this beauty into a mess with an all-hands-on-deck smash. Keep a broom on standby.

SERVES 6 TO 8

INGREDIENTS

Meringues:

4 egg whites

¼ tsp fine sea salt

¼ tsp cream of tartar

⅔ cup sugar

4 cups blackberries

½ cup dessert wine

¼ cup honey

½ tsp ground cinnamon

1 tsp pure vanilla extract

Boozy Fruit Compote:

2 lb/900 g mixed black or purple plums, sliced + seedless concord grapes

Whipped Cream:

1 cup whipping cream

1 Tbsp icing sugar

1 tsp pure vanilla extract

COOK'S NOTE

Feel free to sandwich the 2 meringues together with the filling like a massive dessert sandwich, or make one jumbo, or many mini meringues. For the compote, substitute any fruits in season for the berries, like cherries.

For a quicker dessert, skip the meringues, grease a 10-inch gratin dish, prepare the compote, and bake at 375°F until the fruits are tender and the juices are bubbling, about 20 minutes. Serve over vanilla ice cream or with Lemon Angel Cake (page 250).

Preheat the oven to 225°F. Line 2 baking sheets with parchment paper.

For the meringues, in a stand mixer fitted with the whisk attachment, whip the egg whites on high speed until foamy. Add the salt and cream of tartar and continue to whip on high speed until soft peaks form. Add the sugar and continue to whip on high speed until the whites are stiff and glossy.

Using a spoon, scoop the mixture onto the baking sheets to form 2 large mounds. Use the back of the spoon to swirl and slightly flatten them. You don't need to be too fussy about their shape but try to keep them a similar size.

Bake for 1 to 1½ hours until the meringues are dry, but do not let them change colour. Turn the oven off and, leaving the door ajar, let the meringues cool completely in the oven. You can leave them there overnight or store them in an airtight container at room temperature once they've cooled completely.

For the boozy fruit compote, in a medium saucepan over medium heat, bring the fruits, dessert wine, honey, and cinnamon to a boil, stirring occasionally. Turn down the heat to low and simmer for 10 minutes until the mixture thickens. Stir in the vanilla. Set aside to cool completely.

When ready to serve, in a stand mixer fitted with the whisk attachment, whip the cream with the icing sugar and vanilla on high speed until firm peaks form. Top the meringues with the freshly whipped cream and cooled fruits, leaving them open-faced. Good luck serving—you can attempt to cut the meringue with a chef's knife, but for family fun, allow the kids to give it a smash.

RASPBERRY LEMON SORBET

This is one that my kids can easily make.

SERVES 6

INGREDIENTS

2 cups water

¼ cup sugar

4 cups frozen raspberries

Zest + juice of 2 lemons

¼ cup mint leaves, chopped (optional)

HOW TO

In a small saucepan over medium-high heat, bring the water and sugar to a boil and continue to boil, stirring, for 2 minutes. Let cool in the pan.

In a blender, puree the raspberries with the lemon juice. Strain through a sieve, pressing to remove the seeds. Stir in the cooled syrup, lemon zest, and mint. Pour into an 8-inch square baking pan, or a sheet pan, and freeze for at least 1 hour. Remove from the freezer and let soften for 10 minutes before serving. Store in an airtight container in the freezer for up to a few weeks.

MANGO ORANGE SORBET

This refreshing sorbet can double as freezer pops (see page 262) and can also pass as a breakfast bowl base topped with granola, nuts, and fresh fruit.

SERVES 6

INGREDIENTS

1 cup water

¾ cup maple syrup

3 cups frozen mango chunks

2 oranges, peeled + segmented, pith + seeds removed

Pinch of fine sea salt

Juice of ½ lemon

HOW TO

In a small saucepan over high heat, bring the water and maple syrup to a boil, stirring. Continue to boil, stirring, for 2 minutes until thickened. Set aside to cool to room temperature.

In a blender, puree the cooled syrup with the mango, oranges, sea salt, and lemon juice until completely smooth. Pour into an 8-inch square baking pan, or a sheet pan, and freeze for at least 1 hour. Remove from the freezer and let soften for 10 minutes before serving. Store in an airtight container in the freezer for up to a few weeks.

QUEBEC SUGAR PIE

I had the good fortune of being a judge for the National Magazine Awards. I took the job seriously, and embarked on recipe testing too. The first year I judged, Ricardo won. As a Quebecois cook, he has a few versions of the classic French Canadian sugar pie. He inspired me to create my own, incorporating ideas from my Montreal friend Liz's mom's maple syrup pie, and its store-bought crust, too. This recipe is a sum of all my inspirations. Praise Quebec classic sweets.

MAKES ONE 9-INCH PIE

INGREDIENTS

1 store-bought frozen 9-inch pie shell, thawed

½ cup lightly packed brown sugar

2 Tbsp all-purpose flour

Pinch of fine sea salt

2 eggs

½ cup whipping cream

1 cup maple syrup

1 tsp pure vanilla extract

2 Tbsp butter, cubed

HOW TO

Preheat the oven to 400°F.

In a medium bowl, combine the sugar, flour, and salt.

In a second large bowl, beat the eggs until they are pale yellow. Add the whipping cream and beat until foamy and thickened. Fold in the maple syrup and vanilla extract.

Stir the flour mixture into the egg mixture, until blended and combined. Pour into the unbaked pie crust. Scatter the butter cubes overtop.

Bake for 30 to 40 minutes, until the filling is just set and no longer jiggles. Serve warm with fresh whipped cream or vanilla ice cream.

COOK'S NOTE

I have a major weakness for butter tarts, which can be stocked up and hidden in the freezer. This recipe is in the same vein. My friend Kristi tested it and, as a fellow butter tart fan, insisted this pie tasted best partially frozen. Maybe it's the forbidden element that makes it taste so good.

COOK'S NOTE

*For the Raspberry Lemon Sorbet (above), use fresh raspberries when they're in season,
or keep frozen fruits on hand all year round—they're less expensive and the
fresh ones get gobbled up the second they land in the kitchen.*

*Get creative, and have fun with these sorbets: try different combinations of
fruits and vegetables (strawberry, pineapple, green apple, or spinach), or replace
the water with coconut milk or yogurt. To make Popsicle versions, just divide
the mixture evenly between Popsicle moulds instead of the pan.*

Above: Raspberry Lemon Sorbet, page 260
Right: Mango Orange Sorbet, page 260

SALTED CARAMEL

This one's for the sweet toothed. Yes, there's a lot of sugar and fat in it, but a little salted caramel goes a long way. This recipe is an ideal way to use up any whipping cream you have on hand, or to keep you busy when you're looking for a simple baking distraction. Serve over ice cream like an old-fashioned butterscotch sundae—extra sauce, please—or just enjoy by the spoonful.

MAKES ABOUT 2 CUPS

INGREDIENTS

1 cup packed brown sugar

½ cup cold butter, cubed

½ cup whipping cream

1 tsp pure vanilla extract

1 tsp flaked sea salt

HOW TO

In a small saucepan over medium heat, bring the sugar, butter, and cream to a gentle boil, stirring constantly until slightly thickened and caramel in colour, about 10 minutes. Test if it is ready by taking a small sample of the mixture and dropping it into a glass of cold water; if it forms a soft ball, you know it is ready; if it's not, continue to cook, stirring constantly, for a minute or two. Remove from the heat and stir in the vanilla and salt.

Serve warm over vanilla ice cream. Store in the fridge in a sealed jar for up to a few days if you have that kind of self-control.

KATE'S DATES

My friend Kate (my go-to friend for skiing and also let's-go-out-somewhere-for-a-cocktail) shared this decadent treat, which is now a firm favourite of mine. It combines peanut butter and chocolate—my idea of a perfect pair. The deal was that we'd call the recipe Kate's Dates. It's hard to eat just one.

MAKES 16

INGREDIENTS

16 dates, pitted
¼ cup crunchy peanut butter
  (+ more as needed)

2 cups semisweet chocolate
  chips
Flaked sea salt

HOW TO

Line a baking sheet with parchment paper. Using a sharp knife, cut a slit in each date from end to end to butterfly them. Place them open-side up on the prepared sheet. Fill each date with about 1 teaspoon of peanut butter, pinch the date closed, and return to the baking sheet. Chill in the freezer for 15 minutes.

Bring a medium pot of water to a simmer, place a stainless steel bowl over the pot, and melt the chocolate. Or, in a microwave-safe bowl, melt the chocolate for 1 to 1½ minutes in the microwave. Stir until completely smooth. Set aside to start to cool.

Remove the dates from the freezer. Dip them, one at a time, into the warm, melted chocolate, coating them completely. Return to the baking sheet and sprinkle the top of each date with a pinch of sea salt.

Let the chocolate-covered dates set completely in the fridge until the chocolate is hardened, a few hours. Store in an airtight container in the fridge for up to 5 days.

THANKS

The idea for *My New Table* has been around for years. I suppose it's been a decade in the works. There are many people and places that have inspired me, and contributed to the creation of this book. Collectively, they gave me the nudge I needed to reignite my creativity, so that now I can hold this bucket list project (cookbook #3) in my hands with love, gratitude, and pride.

To Fin, Olivia, and Charlotte. I'm amazed by your resilience and positive energy. You are my fuel—happy kids, happy mom. During a year that tested us collectively beyond comprehension, you carried me with your optimism and energy, and we carried each other. Thank you for trying my recipe creations, giving feedback, and looking at the photos with care and interest as our shared photo album and story unfolded. You are my A-Team.

Mom and Dad, my one stop shop for love, support, and cheerleading. I learned from you that being a parent never ends. We—Tim, Jeff, Robbie, and I, with Nance, Amy, Amanda and Peter, and our large gang of 14 kids—all thank you for being the most invested and involved parents and grandparents we could hope for. We keep you very busy. The valuable skills you brought to the creation of this book are priceless. Mom, my master recipe tester, writer, editor, dishwasher and shared voice; Bobo would be so proud and is smiling down on you. Dad, my eyes on edits, tone and voice, and my trusted creative opinion on style, layout, and design.

Peter, thank you for giving me the support, creative freedom, and time needed to bring this book to life. Thank you for your enthusiasm for my endless collection of pretty platters and expensive produce, and for waking up every morning with a smile and an inspiring work ethic. Connor and Emma, thank you for gobbling up all the works in progress and never complaining.

When I finally felt ready to put this book out into the universe, I thought I should get some help. So I went to Sam Haywood at Transatlantic, and I am grateful for her guidance, calls, and even tears. When I said I needed a photographer who could spend months with me and my family, in our home, on the road, at the farm, help with props, cooking, styling and social media, and more, I knew that would be five different people. But, somehow, it's been just one: Ksenija, photographer extraordinaire and natural stylist. We were a lean team in COVID times. Ksenija, you are a hard worker, multi-tasker, and a talent beyond, and it's been a joy and a lifeline working with a fellow family and country girl. And thank you to my neighbour and friend Alex Younger, who was most generous with his time and camera for those fun country videos.

Meeting with Appetite by Random House was exciting. I had wanted to work with publisher Robert McCullough from my first cookbook *dish entertains* days when he published Donna Hay's books. I sensed we had a shared love and appreciation for the beautiful and, as he says, he "just wants to make a pretty book." Lindsay, you are kind and patient, and I take great comfort in knowing we have a shared vision and are together bringing so much more than a cookbook to life. Katherine, everyone, especially me, needs an editor in their life. Thank you for your patience and for reading my illegible writing. Thank you to Jen for your beautiful design, and for bringing it all to life.

Through the years this book was in the works, I have been lucky to work with some amazing food and lifestyle companies—growing, pivoting or starting up—with inspiring leaders: Indigo and Heather Reisman, Branksome Hall, and Karen Merton, Feast and Steve Harmer, Mama Earth Organics and Alex Billingsley. Thanks also to InvestEco, and to Lynda Reeves of *House & Home* for your support. And to those who helped me pivot my own brand and keep things pretty and relevant: designer Kitty McKechnie, and agency Lux 9's Kate Driscoll and Alexia Wulff.

My thanks to the wonderful store owners whose picks and finds you see pictured in this book. Martha McKimm at Hopson Grace is where I found most of my beautiful tableware and linens, along with Creemore entrepreneur Laurie of Lagom 142 and Heirloom 142; and thank you to Elaine at Kettlewells in Collingwood for her fabulous eye and one-of-a-kind salvage finds. Thank you to my favourite food haunts in Toronto—Summerhill Market; Blackbird Baking Co.; butcher shops Oliffe, St James Town Steak + Chops, Cumbrae's; and Harvest Wagon for the most beautiful produce when our garden is covered in snow. In Creemore, Quince Bistro, Creemore 100 Mile Store, and Bank Café, thank you for feeding me on "cook's night off," and thank you to Catherine at The Creemore Hills Winery for showing me any food dream is possible.

Recipe testers, you are the competent home cooks I trust, and whose tables are similar to mine: Mom, Ksenija, Amanda, aunt Nancy, Kara, Kristi, Ghislaine, and Karen, may this book be our go-to recipe collection for years to come. To my dear old friends Tori, Foofie, Rahat, Bay, and Liz, whose love, laughter, and guidance motivated me to get this done. Also, to my Creemore dinner party friends who set the dinner party bar so high. And to all my fellow cooks, cookbook authors, moms, grandmothers, entrepreneurs, small business owners, growers, and producers, you are my sources of inspiration.

My heart is cracked open with love and appreciation to you all. May this cookbook be part of our story, to enjoy and share through the years to come.

INDEX